Breathing Love

MEDITATION *in* ACTION

JENNIE LEE
Author of *True Yoga*

Llewellyn Worldwide
Woodbury, Minnesota

FIRST EDITION
First Printing, 2018

Book design by Bob Gaul
Cover design by Shira Atakpu

Llewellyn Publications is a registered trademark of Llewellyn Worldwide Ltd.

Library of Congress Cataloging-in-Publication Data
Names: Lee, Jennie, author.
Title: Breathing love: meditation in action / Jennie Lee
Description: First Edition. | Woodbury: Llewellyn Worldwide, Ltd., 2018. |
    Includes bibliographical references and index.
Identifiers: LCCN 2017035231 (print) | LCCN 2017049118 (ebook) |
    ISBN 9780738755168 (ebook) | ISBN 9780738752099 (alk. paper)
Subjects: LCSH: Love. | Meditation. | Yoga. | Love—Religious aspects.
Classification: LCC BF575.L8 (ebook) | LCC BF575.L8 L328 2018 (print) |
    DDC 294.5/48677—dc23
LC record available at https://lccn.loc.gov/2017035231

Llewellyn Worldwide Ltd. does not participate in, endorse, or have any authority or responsibility concerning private business transactions between our authors and the public.

All mail addressed to the author is forwarded, but the publisher cannot, unless specifically instructed by the author, give out an address or phone number.

Any Internet references contained in this work are current at publication time, but the publisher cannot guarantee that a specific location will continue to be maintained. Please refer to the publisher's website for links to authors' websites and other sources.

Llewellyn Publications
A Division of Llewellyn Worldwide Ltd.
2143 Wooddale Drive
Woodbury, MN 55125-2989
www.llewellyn.com

Printed in the United States of America

Disclaimer

The material in this book is not intended as a substitute for trained medical or psychological advice. Readers are advised to consult their personal healthcare professionals regarding treatment. The publisher and the author assume no liability for any injuries caused to the reader that may result from the reader's use of the content contained herein and recommend common sense when contemplating the practices described in the work.

Contents

TO GOD AND GURU
May Thy Love shine forever on the
sanctuary of my devotion. And may
I be able to awaken Thy Love in all hearts.
Paramahansa Yogananda

Introduction

*A truly spiritual person lives for
Truth, and breathes for Love.*
Mata Amritanandamayi (Amma)

Many of us have known love and for this we are blessed. Yet, if you are like me, your capacity to love and to be loved is often tested by the daily trials of life and relationship. With mounting news of hatred, injustice, terrorism, and abuse, our world is in trouble and people are urgently asking, *where* is the love?

If you are ready to accept responsibility for the answer to this question by learning how to shift your consciousness from fear and negativity to faith and trust, this book is for you. If you would like to take a fresh look at what love *is* and what it takes to *live* it beyond personal motive and desire, you have come to the right place. If you are ready to open your heart beyond the constrictions of lack and defensiveness in order to become truly peaceful and powerful, read on.

Inside each of us right here, right now is the greatest love imaginable waiting for us to breathe into it. To access this love, we must move beyond current thought and even emotion to sense the purity of our hearts. Most people do not know how to do this or how to put love into action in their daily lives. We love *some* people *sometimes*, but like the valves of our physical hearts that fluctuate, our ability to express or receive love does as well. This book offers a solution—an action plan for loving in spite of life's difficulties, choosing love *anyway, always,* and *no matter what.*

When it comes to love, everyone—regardless of economic status, educational degree, religion, or even intellect—shares the same potential. The human longing for love is as universal as the human heartbeat. It is as inherent to our being as our breath, and as fundamental to every moment of life. I would go so far as to say that absolutely *everything* in life is related to loving or not loving in some way. We are here to explore how we can approach every situation, person, and experience with open hearts filled with love.

Our journey may seem like a big mountain we must climb, but every expedition begins with a first step, and the payoff for reaching the summit is grand. When we connect to the energy of love within our own beings, the internal void we previously felt is healed, the external seeking is relieved, and all our relationships are transformed. As our hearts open to what is deeper and more powerful than we imagined, fear ceases and we find peace.

My Story

I have always been someone who loved quickly and deeply. A blessing at times, and a curse at others, it was the only way to live that made sense to me. From a young age, I witnessed how fear would stop people from living the lives they truly wanted. In particular, I noticed this fear in my mother. I learned that fear was the only actual thing to fear, and that love was the antidote every time.

For more than thirty years, I have studied world religions and philosophies, seeking a deeper understanding of love. From the Bible to the Tao Te Ching, Buddhist texts, Incan shamanism, and Christian mysticism, I could see a unifying truth in all. The philosophy that spoke most deeply to me was classical Yoga, the path of union, which is descended from ancient Vedic teachings. The Vedas recognize one animating consciousness in all creation, and the ancient yogis sought a personal experience of this through all their physical and spiritual practices. In writing my first book, *True Yoga: Practicing with the Yoga Sutras for Happiness & Spiritual Fulfillment*, I studied numerous translations of the Yoga Sutras, as well as the Bhagavad Gita, the Upanishads, and the spiritual classic, *Autobiography of a Yogi*.

I believe we all share an inherent divinity, and that the Self-realized masters of all spiritual paths and religions have pointed toward love as *the* practice that heals, unites, and evolves human beings. Many traditions recognize meditation as a way of experiencing the sacred or transcendent, so I decided to write this book from a general perspective in the spirit of oneness rather than basing it in a particular tradition.

Other contributing factors to my focus on love and meditation are my study of spiritual psychology and my practice as a yoga therapist for the past twenty years. I have clearly seen a unifying thread between my case studies and clients who have come from vastly differing life histories. The common denominator is that they all deeply need love, and if they were not given a healthy experience of it early in life, they suffer with issues of self-worth and struggle with their interpersonal relationships.

I was fortunate that my personal beginning was one of both healthy attachment and love, for which I am eternally grateful. However, my parents' love did not extend to each other, and I grew up in an environment of battling wills and angry egos fighting for their opinions and agendas. I could not understand how they could profess to love me, yet act so unloving with one another.

I took on the role of mediator in the family, talking to each of my parents separately, trying to get them to understand the other and to be kind. I did not know anything about peace making. I just knew what I needed to feel safe. This impulse has carried on and informed much of my life, defining my personality, career choices, and relational roles. It is why I have written this book, in the hope that I can inspire others to cultivate a relationship with love that transcends individual history, as well as current desires and capacity.

Like everyone else, I have made mistakes in love over my lifetime. I have also seen the miraculous results of how life shifts when we prioritize love with sincerity and devotion. For this reason, I offer personal examples from my journey in every chapter—some lighthearted, some from the darkest and most challenging moments of my life. They illustrate how I developed love as my spiritual practice and the difference it has made to my peace and happiness. My greatest teacher in this has been Paramahansa Yogananda, and it is his writing on the power of conscious loving that took my understanding to a whole new level.

I am well aware that what I share here is not always easy to accomplish. Learning to love wholeheartedly without trying to prove something or get anything in return is not exactly the world standard. It is an act of surrender and nonattachment, meditation in action. I also know that if more people approached loving in this way, the world would be a vastly different place in a very short period of time. What keeps me on this path of opening my heart to love is simply the immeasurable joy I feel when I do.

The Purpose of Life

When my mom was eighty-three and in a nursing home, we had a conversation one day in which she sadly confessed, "I might as well die because I have no purpose." I vehemently countered, "Mom! Your purpose is to love—to love me, your friends, and these people here around you. How can there be any greater purpose than that? It does not matter what you *do* for someone, as much as how you show them love." She stared out at the flower garden and contemplated this for a while.

When I visited her next, she introduced me to her new friend Charlotte, a Nigerian woman who was a nurse's aid. Charlotte barely spoke English but she clearly had a connection with my mom. What was most interesting about this new friendship was that my mom had struggled her whole life with a severe prejudice against people of other races. Yet she had taken my words to heart and now was holding this woman's hand and calling her a friend. *Practicing love is life changing.*

What to Expect

Wherever you are in life—in a relationship or not, in your prime or nearing death, you will find support in these pages to awaken a new level of love in your heart. Here are tools to help you break through the pain, pride, and fear that have made you suffer and kept you alienated from the love you long for.

In part one, we begin by sorting out the differences between human love and divine love, reframing the entire concept of what true love is. We examine the obstacles we may encounter as we try to love bigger and explore practices to clear out these roadblocks. We approach the karmic release and forgiveness necessary for a clean experience in human love relationship. We discover that pain does not have to be the only catalyst for change; love well-lived has the potential to heal us and give our lives great meaning through both giving and receiving.

We establish a simple practice of meditation that consciously brings us back again and again to heart opening and the joy inherent in breathing love.

In part two, we look at how to gain a deeper experience of love *within* ourselves so that we can rely less on the partial expressions of love from other struggling humans. We look at the richness of transition times (up to and including death) to overcome identification with the body we inhabit, and thereby know ourselves as the soul *inhabiting* the body ever connected to love. We examine how love can soften the effects of grief and loss. Finally, we determine what it takes to create a new reality based on love today and how to leave a legacy of love behind when we go.

Suggestions for daily practice are offered at the end of each chapter. Many of the meditations are "off the cushion" so to speak—practices that make our lives a continual meditation. Additional self-reflective exercises help create an action plan of loving that moves us through life with intention and ease. The appendices provide extended meditations, affirmations, and prayers to support the ongoing journey of living love every day.

Take your time and work through the book in a way that makes sense to you. Read the sections that call your heart first and do the exercises that feel most important for your journey in this moment.

It is never too early (nor too late) to begin this life-changing spiritual practice, for if we learn to love *totally,* even for a moment, we will be forever enriched. Eventually practicing love becomes as natural as breathing, and life becomes full of joyful purpose. It is my hope that you will be inspired and share my conviction to breathe love at every turn and no matter what life brings, love *anyway*.

PART ONE

· · · · · · · · · · · ·

Clearing Space

· · · · · · · · · · · ·

Choose love, and you are being proactive:
you are making things happen, living a life
of choice, and getting better. Choose fear,
and you are being reactive: you are letting things
happen, living a life of chance, and getting bitter.
Phil Bolsta

Summary

To align ourselves with love, we need to purge the pain, pride, and fear that restrict us and taint our understanding of our true nature. Maybe you are tired of experiencing the same pain year after year, or maybe you just sense that there must be more to love than you have experienced so far. By releasing, trusting, forgiving, and awakening the remembrance of ourselves *as* love through both seated and active meditation practices, we learn to give and receive in new and expansive ways, bringing immense joy into every day.

Chapter One

....

Love and the Search
for Inner Peace

... Think not you can direct the course of love,
for love, if it finds you worthy, directs your course.
Love has no other desire but to fulfill Itself.
Kahlil Gibran

Throughout human history, love has been ubiquitously sung about, continuously analyzed, and often misunderstood. From poets to mystics, school children to senior citizens, religious leaders to advertising executives, everyone is searching for the magic elixir to enlighten, inspire, and satisfy our insatiable desire. To love and to be loved is the greatest motivator, from the moment we are born until the moment we die, an ever-renewing incentive.

As babies, we learn that whoever satisfies our physical needs is essential for our survival. If we were lucky, these providers loved us and saw that we were emotionally nurtured as well as physically fed. As a result, we associate love from *others* as essential and assume that the people who love us are the fundamental *source* of love. We spend the rest of our lives searching for the satisfaction of our needs outwardly through other human beings. Invariably this takes us on a circuitous journey through countless relationships that lead at best to partial fulfillment and disappointment and delusion more often than not.

The Nature of the Game

Because love is packaged in alluring ways to trigger our hardwired longing for fulfillment, it is quite easy to find ourselves caught in the trap of wanting love completely, but finding it impossible to attain. Because we need love so much, we seek it in ever new and distorted ways, chasing passions and believing that if we satisfy enough of them, we will be filled. It is not until we understand the fundamental difference between personal love and universal love that we will be free of this pursuit. To understand this difference and how it affects our daily experience is an essential part of our journey together.

We begin at the surface of things with personal love. Driven by our egos and influenced by desire, this level of love fluctuates based on our feelings in any given moment. In contrast, universal love constantly flows to whomever is in its path. It is deep, pure, and more profound than any personal sentiment can convey. It is expressed through acts of selfless service, kind words, and general goodwill to all humankind. It is felt as patience, truthfulness, trust, hope, and perseverance. Universal love holds no fear, pride, envy, or anger. It sees no faults, weaknesses, or differences.

But love itself is even more than any of the qualities or qualifications I have mentioned. Love is energy, the raw energy that comprises the very fabric of the universe. It is the attractive principle permeating every part of creation, always drawing us back to itself for completion. In essence, love is the fullness of life expressed.

The energy of love is singular in essence yet infinite in manifestation. It is differentiated and perceived in innumerable ways depending on the human consciousness it is flowing through. What we experience as personal love in all its varying forms is always an offshoot of Source love, just different in level and degree.

Self Versus self

When our souls come into bodily form, the one energy or consciousness that comprises the universe has the experience of being separate and unique. The force that creates this experience is called *maya* in Sanskrit, and is described as a veil of illusion that makes us believe we are different and incomplete, therefore needy of the love of others to make us whole. Maya is the dividing force of creation in opposition to love, the unifying force.

Because of maya, we experience duality: dark and light, good and evil, self and other. Maya causes us to identify with the personal self (lowercase s) as differentiated from the soul or universal Self (capital S). Personal love is associated with the small s self, representing the human personality and its individualized loving. Universal love comes from the soul or capital S Self, the one consciousness of which we are all a part.

When souls become embodied, they temporarily forget that they are a part of the unified spiritual Self. The force of maya divides and disharmonizes, stripping us of the memory of being innately divine, made of love, and worthy of love regardless of race, nationality, sexual orientation, or religious belief. We then spend our lives trying to get oriented and form connections in this physical plane, yet forever feel that there is something missing.

Me, Myself, and I

Engaging with the world through the limited filter of small s self, we operate from an I/me/mine perspective and often feel disconnected from the Source of love, wisdom, and truth. When we are in this state of delusion, we feel ungrounded, anxious, and afraid, like we do not fit in. We fear rejection and strive for greater achievements to prove our worth. We judge and compare, criticize and manipulate, overanalyze, worry, and react emotionally, all in an effort to hold onto personal love. And because we believe we are separate and distinct from one another, we spend a great deal of time in self-preservation indulging, defending, and protecting our small self's identity.

Do those behaviors sound familiar? We all experience these things to a greater or lesser degree daily. The endless stories of suffering associated with human relationships prove that this egocentric small self is the state of consciousness we operate from most of the time, and we do not experience pure love because of it. We are disconnected from the sacred presence of love within us—it is a spiritual disease that affects us personally and collectively.

Because we believe that we are separate, we serve self-interest over others' well-being and judge and condemn those around us. The small, separate self fluctuates between confusion, emotionalism, and isolation. It fears loss, lacks trust, and is often possessive. The following list further defines how the small self operates.

- Concentrates on anything self-referential, the "I," "me," or "my"

- Senses limitations which induce fear, neuroses or hopelessness

- Fluctuates between feeling powerful and powerless

- Indulges desires, addictions, impulses, and habits

- Seeks fulfillment in the physical/temporary rather than the spiritual/ eternal

- Is strongly attached to the body, even near death

- Relies upon information rather than intuition

- Compares itself to others

- Judges and criticizes self and others

- Projects, shames, manipulates, and instills guilt

- Is confused and unable to make clear decisions

- Is reactive, easily triggered, and defensive

- Is fueled by self-doubt and fear

- Feels alone and separate

Every egocentric tendency keeps us from the light of our infinite nature and we suffer as a result of this perceived separation. Until we reclaim the awareness of our true Self as love, our souls will remain disenfranchised and afraid, bumping into other souls equally as fearful and lost. We will be continually disappointed in our efforts to find love, no matter how many relationships we enter.

So the first step in learning how to better love and be loved is to change our self-perception. It is time to liberate our consciousness from the identification of self as strictly human, struggling with the ups and downs of life. Our souls have become completely associated with these individual bodies, so we must remind them that their original divine nature *is* love. By shifting from the false belief that we are the temporary vehicle (the body) to the remembrance of our soul's divine origin and inherent nature as love, we begin healing our aching hearts. It does not help to hate ourselves in our suffering or to surround hate-filled people with more animosity—such actions only increase the power of maya's delusion.

To awaken from the spiritual ignorance we all share, the only solution—inwardly or outwardly—is love. If we or people we know are currently experiencing self-loathing, judgment, or negativity, we must remember that the divine energy of love is hidden right behind these veils of delusion, just waiting to be coaxed back out through compassion and forgiveness. If we do not, we will fall deeper and deeper into our beliefs of separation. More on how to remember our true nature follows in later chapters, but for now let us get really clear about the nature of the ego self and how it wreaks havoc on our personal experience of love.

The Personality in Love

Because of the delusive force of maya, most human relationships are based on allegiance to the ego self and are therefore quite selfish. In intimate relationships, our tendency is to see through the I/me/mine perspective and to act for our personal agendas. Even at the beginning of a new relationship, when we think we have fallen in love with another, what is often happening is that we are reacting to what the other person is giving us in terms of attention, affection, or validation. It feels good, so we associate that with love. We want more, so we give in order to get.

Inevitably, time passes and we stop getting exactly what we want so we no longer *feel* loved; in return, we stop loving. We feel hurt and react out of our fear, condemnation, shame, or pride. Friction ensues, hearts close, and relationships end. We may move on to a new love connection, and for a while it might seem better, but then the same pattern comes into play.

All relationships, from the seemingly insignificant to the most intimate, are opportunities to free ourselves from the delusion of separateness and the agendas of the ego. When we can do this, even to a small degree, everything changes. Maya loses its grip and we experience the fluctuations of human loving with more levity and empathy, rather than with fear and self-criticism.

Living Love

The very key to our freedom lies in the active *practice of loving*. In order to reconnect with our souls, we must learn to *live* as the love that we *are*. In contrast to the small self's mode of operation, when we live from our expansive soul nature, we feel open, peaceful, harmonious, and accepting of life's flow, because our happiness does not depend on other people or on outer circumstances. By remembering our shared divine heritage, we shift ourselves out of selfishness and the limitations of personal love.

This change can begin today. It is as easy as practicing simple acts of thoughtfulness, offering a genuine smile or greeting to the person waiting on us in the check out line, or serving us food at a restaurant. If we live in service to universal love *through* one another thinking in terms of "we" and not "I," we immediately start to feel more connected.

By actively embodying qualities such as peacefulness, truthfulness, patience, kindness, self-control, and appreciation, we revitalize our hearts. We feel a new sense of worth, one that is stronger than the inner critic pulling us back into a limited view of self. By becoming generous in spirit, we enrich our lives as well as others. The following are examples of how the soul Self operates.

- Handles what life brings with ease
- Lives from highest values, even in difficult situations
- Bears witness to the endless rise of the ego's desires without indulging them
- Remains unattached to particular outcomes
- Determines actions based on whether they foster peace in the present moment
- Knows there is ultimately nothing to lose and therefore nothing to defend
- Expresses unselfish love even when others disappoint
- Recognizes the interconnectedness of all beings
- Enters relationships focused on what we can give rather than get
- Handles conflict through self reflection rather than blame
- Contributes to the spiritual evolution of others

Connected to our soul Self, we know that we are individualized expressions of infinite love, operating a physical and mental body to relate in this finite world. When we witness our ego's tendency toward nonloving, heart-closing behavior, we compassionately draw ourselves back to the truth that we are souls; whole, wise, peaceful, happy, powerful, humble, intuitive, and filled with joy. Instead of looking for what we can get from others or what we feel they owe us in terms of love, we open the heart again and again into its natural state of purity.

In order to live from our soul Self all the time, we need a way to quiet the emotional fluctuations of the human heart. Meditation is the way. It creates an essential pause in which we can reconnect to our innately peaceful nature. In the next chapter, we explore meditation in its traditional seated form, as well as a living, breathing practice to employ in daily life.

Meditation aligns our hearts with love. The more we practice, the happier we become, and the better life gets. It is a brilliantly simple equation and yet although it is simple, there are a million reasons why it is incredibly difficult to put into action. If it were easy, we would already be doing it. We dare not remain forgetful. It is time for change.

A Personal Story

The morning of my thirtieth birthday, I awoke with concerned thoughts about where my life was heading. I was living in Los Angeles at the time, married, no kids, pursuing a career in the entertainment industry as an actor and screenwriter. I had met moderate success and was supporting myself solely through acting gigs, but I was feeling little fulfillment. I craved more meaning in my work than smiling for a salad dressing advertisement. The screenplays I had written were filled with positive messages about human relationships and love, but had received little attention from producers. I wanted to get a message of hope and joy out to the world in contrast to the violence and greed I saw portrayed in most media. But intuitively I sensed that it was not yet my time. I thought I needed more life under my belt to be able to write these messages from a place of greater authority.

Looking back now, I realize that although my intentions were good, at that time I wanted success for *me*. I had something to prove to myself, my family, and the world. *I* (i.e., my small self) had a message and was intent on making a difference. In my mind, I rationalized that this was a worthy effort undertaken in the spirit of love. It might have been, sure, but it was still anchored in ego. The twenty-year journey that followed has helped me shift to a more soul-centered perspective.

A few years later I decided to walk away from the entertainment industry when my first child was born. After a couple of stay-at-home years, I turned my professional focus to the world of yoga, opening a studio and creating a private yoga therapy practice. But a decade and a half later, feeling much of the same frustration I had felt in the world of acting, I realized that my ego was still the thing getting in the way of my true happiness. No matter how hard I worked, how lofty the goal I achieved, or how much I believed in my mission as a teacher, I still felt unsatisfied and like I had not done *enough*. I was looking for an outer return on my efforts at helping people that would give me inner validation. I felt disillusioned and despaired of ever making a dramatic difference in the world. What I know now is that both disillusionment and despair are signs of the ego having a tantrum.

In 2014, my work all but dried up, and I questioned whether I was meant to teach anymore. Broken down by more ego-slaughtering rejection than I could imagine, I finally surrendered the outcome of all my efforts to love. This was a painful process of letting go of all attachment to the results of my work and all identification with success or failure based on my actions. At the same time, I had to be willing to keep showing up day after day to whatever was in front of me to do. For example, after owning a thriving yoga studio for ten years, I spent a year teaching at other people's studios, often having only one or two people show up to my classes. I stayed because I knew that my ego was being chipped away and that this was what needed to happen in order to reconnect to my soul. When I finally reached the state of honest nonattachment to what I might get from my work, the ego climbed into the passenger seat, and my soul finally got a chance to drive.

Outwardly, not much changed. I still got up every day and did my meditation practice as well as any outreach I could think of to expand my business. But inwardly I felt a shift, a loosening of the grip of personal desire. I had let go and really surrendered in my heart the results of all of my efforts. I trusted that whatever was meant to be mine would be mine. And whatever was not would not, and that it was all okay. I released the beliefs that I needed to be a nationally recognized teacher, published writer, or guest on *Oprah* in order to make a difference. I relinquished the desire to make a million dollars or change the world in a dramatic way. I did what I could each day for my circle of family, friends, and clients. I rested in love.

Several things happened because of my shift in thinking. I felt more peaceful. I enjoyed my days more. I became most entertained by watching how my ego would try to reclaim its position in charge at every possible opportunity, rearing its attitudes of righteousness, comparison, jealousy, and self-pity when things were not going my way. When we can take ourselves lightly, this lifelong battle between the ego and the soul becomes priceless comedy. Amazingly, after seven years of rejections, I received my first book contract for *True Yoga*, which enabled me to fulfill a long-held dream of sending a message of positivity and love into the world.

I would not change a day of the journey. Every day teaches me more about how to live love. For this I am grateful, because love is life's most precious gift.

Daily Practices

Tuning In

In order to notice the difference between the small self and its efforts *in* love and the greater Self and its essence *as* love, we need to practice periods of stillness throughout the day. These are moments to check in, get centered, self-reflect. They are moments to manage stress, to listen to our inner needs, and to respond with self-compassion.

Begin by creating a strong habit of relaxation throughout the day. Whenever you think of it, take a deep breath and tense the whole body. Then exhale, release the tension, and completely relax. After a few repetitions of this, notice the quality of your breath. Is it shallow, grasping, or held back in any way? Try to deepen it and even it out, allowing more space for love.

Ego versus Soul Exercise

Review the qualities of the ego self and the soul Self from this chapter. Begin to notice how much of the I/me/mine perspective runs your day. Then consider the following questions:

- Do I hold any beliefs about love that are not uplifting to me?

- Do I have any judgments about love? About myself and love? About others and love?

Notice if your answers came from your ego or your soul. How do these feel different? Do not worry if you feel a bit unsettled by this; it is normal as we transition between old beliefs and new understandings.

Love Energization Exercise

Rub your palms together until you generate heat. Separate the hands slightly as though holding a small ball. Hold this ball of energy in front of your heart. Think of it as the energy of love. Then extend your hands and send it out to someone specific who you know needs love. Rub the palms again stimulating love and then extend your hands, offering it to the world at large. Rub the hands together once again and hold the ball of energy at your heart center. Then pull it into yourself, placing both hands over the heart. Take a moment to feel the love.

Chapter Two

....

Beginning Meditation
on Love

In meditation when the mind
becomes absorbed in the One... you
become filled with Divine Love, which
overflows to all—not a possessive love,
but a love that is freeing.

Daya Mata

All traditions and styles of meditation have benefits physical, mental, emotional, and spiritual. For the purposes of
expanding our experience of love, there is no greater way than
to establish both a dedicated sitting practice of meditation
and one that is organically interwoven throughout our lives.
We need meditation now more than ever to overcome the
spiritual dementia that keeps us suffering and alienated from
love. In the stillness created through meditation, we learn to

unplug from the sensory experience of the ego self and reconnect with our souls.

Even the tiniest turning back toward our soul nature helps us feel more settled and at peace here and now, and more inclined to be kind to those around us. Whether we know it or not, we all yearn to end our self-imposed exile from love. Meditation helps us make our way through the darkness of delusion in our own hearts, to the remembrance that we already *are* that which we are seeking. The practice offers us a direct experience of unified reality, and sparks a greater capacity for loving.

The Way Out Is In

In order to perceive our shared divine essence, we need a container for the resentment, fear, temptation, sorrow and disappointment that we all struggle with. We need to befriend the hurt feelings that come through our misguided attempts at love, in order to move beyond them into a genuine experience of true love. But how do we keep our hearts open and access love if we have been wounded? How can we awaken love in others who are closed as a result of painful abuse or neglect? We need a space in which we can transform pain and experience a new level of love.

Meditation creates this space in which we can observe our consciousness and balance the interplay of the small ego self and the pure soul Self. By cultivating inner stillness, we create a calm foundation that allows the ego to relax, and the soul to take charge, providing loving guidance for our lives. We quiet our fluctuating feelings and learn to watch but not follow our restless thoughts.

Through meditation we counteract the damaging effects of anxiety, anger, and stress in our lives and build the strength to overcome self-defeating habits. We develop the ability to be in positive, fulfilling relationships, and we connect to personal meaning and purpose. With consistent practice, we widen the channel of our awareness so the fullness of Source love might flow through us continuously without obstructions.

Inner and Outer Practice

Like love, meditation can be practiced by anyone, anywhere, anytime, regardless of religion, age, or health status. It requires no material resources for success and no prior experience. To meditate, the first requirement is simply the will to move into stillness and inquire within. We must detach from the continuously stimulating outer world and stop offering all our time and attention to external pursuits of love to come into communion with it within. Both meditating and loving begin as conscious actions first and then evolve into permanent states of being.

Meditation Tips

For any meditation practice to be effective, the same things are needed: consistency, focus, devotion, and surrender. With consistent meditation comes deep inner peace. With focus comes a quiet mind. From devotion, the heart melts open. And from the ego's surrender, the inner wellspring of joy and wisdom can bubble through us, igniting the divine spark within.

To have the most positive experience possible in a formal seated practice of meditation, consider these practical suggestions. Create a dedicated space in your environment that is just for your quiet time, even if it is only a small corner of a room. Energy is generated through repetitive action in a place, and by cultivating stillness on a daily basis in a particular spot, you will begin to feel an energetic support every time you go there.

Have a small ritual for your time of meditation. For instance, read an uplifting quotation, light a candle, or offer a prayer. Prepare the body for sitting by tensing all the muscles and then releasing and relaxing completely, like in the Tuning In exercise at the end of chapter one. Once seated, maintain an erect spine to enable the free flow of energy.

Turn your internal gaze upward toward the point between the eyebrows, known as the third eye or center of wisdom and intuition, in order to intentionally shift toward higher awareness. Allow your breath to move naturally and easefully in and out.

Focus your mind on an aspect of love that is most dear to you, such as divine mother, beloved friend, or creative flow. Anytime thought wanders, gently bring your concentration back to this focal point.

By withdrawing from worldly distractions and focusing one-pointedly on love, the mind eventually stops racing and becomes like a clear lake, where we can see reflected our true nature. By disciplining our attention and cultivating a commitment to meditate with love, we soon find ourselves becoming more peaceful. The key is to always enter meditation with a joyful heart, relax, and absorb yourself in love.

The Progression of Meditation

A regular practice of sitting meditation builds the capacity to become an impartial witness to our internal experience. Then we can recognize when and how we block the free flow of love energy. This is not an intellectual process but an awareness that awakens from within our hearts through meditation. Love cannot be experienced through the intellect, because reason is a limited instrument of our senses, and love is the unlimited energy of our being. We experience truth and love, not through intellectual or sensory reasoning, but through receptivity in meditation.

Over time, the practice increases our calmness. Things that used to trigger us and make us upset are not as emotionally compelling as they once were. We spend less time judging people or circumstances as well as defending our position or opinions. We notice the ego's jockeying for its selfish motives and choose not to indulge it. We are able to bring our mind under control and understand life from an intuitive state of perception.

The more we meditate, the more we remain connected to our soul Self. The wounded and closed parts of our hearts heal. We release personal expectations and attachments, and feel lighthearted and integrated mentally and emotionally. With consistent practice, we begin to dis-identify with the body and act from our inherent divinity.

This is the reunification of personal consciousness, with our higher Self or love consciousness, as described in sacred texts as unified awareness or enlightenment. When we realize that we are in fact love itself, we recognize that we cannot possibly be without it or separate from it.

Eventually inner calmness transforms into a steady, unshakable joy, one that is totally different from the pleasure we feel at the satisfaction of external desires. This joy is the effect of love, and it is felt physiologically and psychologically in the epicenter of the heart. As it bubbles up within us, we are compelled to do more good in the world. Reactivity is replaced by fearless compassion, and eventually we feel love for all beings as completely as we do for own dearest loved ones. Then we are able to offer unconditional love to others even if they cannot return the same.

Begin With This Breath

Maybe everything you've read so far sounds too good to be true and impossible to achieve. That is okay. We can only be where we are in this moment in our experience and our understanding. If you would like to move toward this realization of your true nature as love, you can start where you are now. Start by taking a breath, your next breath, into love.

Try it. Breathe love in and breathe love out. It is all around you, the energy of the Universe. It is the essential life force within you that you exchange with everyone and everything around you. Nothing and no one can keep you from it and nothing and no one can bring it to you from outside. Try it again. Breathe in love. Breathe out love. Repeat, again and again. It is really so simple.

Breath is the essence of life. By intentionally breathing love, we change our physical, mental, and emotional experience of loving. Affirm with each inhalation and each exhalation that love is who you *are*. You do not have to wait for anything or anyone to do this. Every moment of every day, we have the choice and can immediately reap benefits from the first conscious breath we take in love. This can be a lifetime or more of effort… or in this very instant you can know that you *are* love. You cannot be otherwise.

Self-Realization

As we move beyond thought, words, and ideas, to the experience of true Self in meditation, we realize that we are not just mortal, but absolutely one with the omnipresence of love. We know that we are not separate from it, have never been separate from it and can never be anything but one *with* it. All longing in our hearts for personal love, all the loneliness and inner emptiness, all that we desire is satisfied when our soul returns to this original state of being. Then we feel an absolute trust in the unfolding of our lives. This experience and awareness of love is the greatest result of meditation and is called Self-realization.

Is this the end of the story? I suppose it could be if we actually did this with every breath. But there is much in our lives that makes embracing this simple practice a challenge. In the chapters to come, we will explore the obstacles to loving at this level. The challenge is high but the reward is great, so read on, and have faith. By learning to love beyond your personal self, aligned with Source love, you are calling in peace and joy beyond your wildest imaginings.

A Personal Story

My son asked me the other day if I could receive the answer to any question about spirituality, what would I want to know? I did not hesitate in my response; I wanted to know if meditation will ever get any easier!

I have taught meditation for more than a decade and maintained a daily personal practice. I also lead a weekly meditation group and hear my students' frustrations about beginning and sustaining their practices. We all seem to struggle with the same things, the pressures of time, difficulty focusing and quieting the mind, and doubt that we are making any significant progress. The reason we all struggle is because our ego minds refuse to let go and be quiet. Even after all these years, although I have established meditation as a definite habit and commitment in my life and I do feel results, I still struggle almost daily to relax, settle in, and enjoy the experience. So if you have tried and been frustrated, I understand and encourage you to please not give up.

As I reflected further on my son's query, I realized that what would help me most is not a guarantee that meditation will get easier with another month, year, or decade of practice. What I really need is to accept that like most worthwhile things in life, meditation may never be easy, but if I can love the challenge and trust the process, the results will be right there for me.

In fact, in the moments when my busy mind goes still, I feel such balance, love, and a sense of security knowing that everything is okay and that everything else ceases to matter. I have to remember to be grateful for those glimmers, however fleeting, and concentrate on them rather than on the moments that feel lacking. The same is true for love. We may not feel it all the time, but the moments when we do tap into it are precious and priceless, worth all the effort that has been invested.

I asked a dear friend of mine who has helped me often in times of need what I could do for him. He responded, "Just keep meditating." I chuckled but totally got his meaning. When I reconnect with my true Self in meditation I become a much more thoughtful and compassionate person in the world, and it benefits not just my friend but also everyone around me. Will you do the same? Join me in the sanctuary of stillness where we reconnect to one another and to love.

Daily Practices

Creating the Habit of Meditation

Establish a daily routine of seated meditation, even if it is just five to ten minutes. Set up a small space where you will come each day to develop your practice. Review the meditation tips in this chapter. Done consistently, even a short practice will yield results in peace and clarity. Make this as regular as brushing your teeth each morning and evening, and feel the effects of reconnecting to love.

Breathing Love Meditation

The breath reflects the opening and closing of our hearts in each moment. To cultivate inner peace, place one hand over your heart, and let the other hand rest open in your lap. Begin to take conscious breaths of love. Breathe in deeply and close the hand on your lap. Feel the simultaneous receiving of the breath and receiving of love. Then breathe out, open your hand, and feel the simultaneous offering through the breath and offering of love out into the world through your hand. Continue for several minutes and recognize the interplay between giving and receiving love through every breath. Every breath I exhale in love, you inhale. Every exhalation you offer in love, I inhale. Together we can change the world, one breath at a time.

Love Awareness Meditation

Lie down comfortably and pay attention to your natural breath. Notice the quality of the breath, its length, depth, evenness, sound, and consistency. Notice where you feel it and how. Then tune in to your heart center and the love you feel there. Notice the quality of your love in this moment, its length, depth, evenness, sound, and consistency. Notice where and how you feel love. Now try to deepen the breath. Feel the connection between the sea of breath around you and within you. Allow more in. Then try to deepen your awareness of love. Feel the connection between the love around you and within you. Allow more in. Rest in love for five to ten minutes.

Chapter Three

·························

Temptation and Desire:
Love in Disguise

*The ego attempts to satisfy through
material channels the soul's constant,
insatiable longing for God.*

Paramahansa Yogananda

As soon as we begin meditation, we recognize how restless our minds are. We continuously jump from one thought or feeling to the next, and a majority of this fluctuation has to do with the things we do or do not want. From when we wake up until we sleep, the mind seeks fulfillment of physical, mental, and emotional pleasure and reacts to its gratification or lack thereof. As soon as one yearning is satisfied, the mind is tempted by another because the indulgence of sensory-based pleasures only ever brings a transient moment of happiness. Nothing outside fulfills us forever. However, when the

41

mind's cravings are not quenched, the ego gets upset and goes on chasing the dream.

We are literally propelled through life by our desires, and the skillful rationalizing mind that convinces us we should pursue the enjoyment of them all in order to be happy. This is particularly true about the desire for love. Driven by our ego's selfishness, we strive to protect what we want and get rid of what we do not. It conveniently ignores consequences that might be harmful to others or to us, or it twists the facts in its own favor. Sadly, the modern world encourages the narcissistic self to see things only as they relate to its personal needs and desires.

In truth, desires are poor guides for living life and cultivating real love. Far from paving the road to joy, they often cause us to stray further from what will enable lasting fulfillment. What we *want* may make us happy in the moment but its effect is not enduring.

Because desire is fleeting, we must rethink our relationship with it so that temptation will not sabotage our journey to true love. If we do not, then we will surely go the way of many exalted teachers who have fallen from grace by sating their sexual appetites with students or securing their financial stability through donations. If we practice overcoming our ego nature by tempering the cravings that drive our days, and mastering desire rather than letting it control us, we can attain peace within and remain connected to our innate joy, even when we are not receiving it from external relationships.

Pitfalls of Pleasure

To gain control of desire, we must call our personal pleasure traps into clear view. We all have something in the material world that is particularly alluring—our kryptonite, so to speak. It could be a couple of nightly drinks, television binging, obsessive exercising, or the compulsion to lie to get our way. For some it may be work, sexual fantasies, or prestigious possessions. Temptation pulls at us every day, screaming for our attention like an inconsolable baby until we feed it. Fed enough times, however, it becomes habit, and habit-driven desires become ensnarements. If not escaped, these become addictions, things we turn to so that we may sustain ourselves when life feels stressful or unfulfilling. It is hard to admit that we are all addicts to something.

We reclaim our power when we place our pleasure traps in the light of acceptance and understanding, because true love is to temptation as light is to darkness. In the presence of one, the other disappears. If left in the dark, any selfish desire, shame, or failure will drag us down by dictating to our subconscious and creating an energetic block. Likewise, anything within our consciousness that is harmful can be overcome if it is brought into the light and loved into transformation.

Soul Longing

When we dig a bit deeper, to the root of all human craving, we find the longings of the soul. Every desire we harbor has a counterpart in our soul's quest for remembrance of its

infinite nature. It is essential that we direct these soul longings appropriately, so they do not corrupt into cravings and
addictions that pull us deeper into identification with the ego
rather than our spiritual nature.

Desire can be categorized into eight deep longings of the
soul. They are freedom, power, beauty, wisdom, security, creativity, joy, and love. If we can identify the essential soul yearning, then we can shift the power that desire holds over our lives.
Consider the following examples.

The desire to blow off work and play is essentially the
soul's desire to experience freedom and its unlimited nature.
The desire to manipulate others for personal gain is the soul's
desire for its innate omnipotence. The desire to feel attractive
is the soul's desire for its inherent brilliance, light, and grace.
The desire for knowledge in any form is the soul's desire for its
natural omniscience. The desire for money and other forms of
physical security is the soul's desire for its peaceful perfection
independent of anything external. The desire for worldly success is essentially the soul's desire to express its infinite creativity. The desire for anything pleasing to the senses is the soul's
desire for its native joy. And at the foundation of all the above
is love, the greatest longing of the human heart and soul.

If we are able to see the soul striving to satisfy its longings via the self, we build some perspective around the ways
in which desire runs our days. Then we can break the cycle
of being propelled by desire into things that do not serve our
highest good.

Gaining Control Over Desires

To begin, we need to become witness to the endless selfishness of the senses and regulate desire by consciously choosing *not* to indulge every whim or habit. In this way, we maintain control over desire rather than allowing it to control us. By recognizing the ego in its many iterations in daily life and choosing not to pander to it, we can shift from a self-referential worldview into a more soul-centered perspective, and feel greater joy in our lives and in our relationships. Of course there are some high level desires, ones that take us closer to love, but we must remain unattached even to those.

In order to gain power over our habits and addictions, we need self-control to resist temptation. The instinctual brain reverts to what is known and what is easiest. But although indulgence of desire may taste sweet at first, true joy depends on being able to do what our intuitive wisdom tells us we *should* do. We are only truly free when we no longer operate on the autopilot of habit.

To do this we must be discriminative about the environments and relationships that support, rather than sabotage, our will. We cannot expect to remain strong *and* mix with people who have the same negative tendencies or habits we are trying to break. We must get out of temptation's way and employ strong reason. Every action originates in thought, so we must watch our mental environment as well, recognizing that our thoughts can either elevate or degrade us.

Through our meditation practice, we learn to observe the fluctuations of the mind and tune in to a quieter place of intuitive discrimination from which we can make healthier choices. With intuition turned on, we can assess *why* we are about to do something, and note what the soul is seeking below the outer desire. Once we perceive our soul's true longing, we can employ the necessary "will" power or "won't" power to overcome temptation.

Train Your Brain

The discipline of cultivating even-mindedness during meditation is our key to getting off the seesaw of desire. Even the smallest amount of meditation, or one that does not feel particularly peaceful, increases our self-control afterwards. Although you may not notice results during your meditation time, pay attention to how it affects the rest of your day. Intensified practice increases impulse control, concentration, the ability to manage stress, and self-awareness.

Every time we catch ourselves moving away from a positive direction and point ourselves back, we put the higher Self in charge and willpower rises. We do not need to suppress desire as much as we need to develop conscious control over it, and we do this by staring temptation in the eye and naming it as the saboteur to our happiness that it is. It is not enough to forgo desires to spare ourselves sorrow or the humiliation of failure to achieve them. Relinquishing desires must be based on a full commitment to serve love.

Non-Attached Passion

You might wonder, if we lessen or get rid of our desires, are we not electing a dull existence? What will motivate us? The answer depends on our understanding of nonattachment.

Strongly held desires usually lead to attachment, and although attachment is touted by Western psychology as necessary for love, it is actually its sure demise. Consider that when we desire something or someone, it is often for what the object brings to us. Like picking a flower to keep rather than admiring its beauty and letting it be, we are loving ourselves more than we are loving the other. If we remain in this self-centered paradigm through which we see things or people only as they relate to our needs or desires, then relationship is simply commerce, where supply and demand will naturally fluctuate. But if we go beyond our flirtation with desire into what is real, we find a love that is beyond attachment, beyond likes and dislikes, beyond pleasure and pain. Only here can we learn to love people as they are rather than as we want or need them to be.

Emotional bonds of attachment form when we place reliance for our happiness on the presence of another person or thing, and it sets us up for suffering because everything in the physical realm is temporary. When the relationship ends, the project fails, or the person dies, it is our attachment that causes pain. It keeps us in a cycle of perpetual unhappiness, wandering through the material world longing for that which is essentially spiritual in nature.

It is necessary that we not mistake temptation, desire, or attachment (which are by their nature compulsive, limiting, and self-centered) for real love. Pure love is eternal, limitless, and impersonal. True passion—the spiritual impulse to create and expand—can only bloom when selfish attachment is released.

By quieting the fluctuations of emotions and the restlessness of the mind through meditation, we tune in to intuitive guidance and discern whether a desire contributes to our ability to know our spiritual Self as love or not. We track whether we are on the right path by the level of peace and non-attachment we feel. When we can honestly say, "May this or something greater be for the highest good of all involved," we are on the road to true joy. Any desire that disturbs our peace of mind is a test, showing us the weak link in our consciousness where we need to pour in more love.

We do not need to be at the mercy of our emotions, cravings, and impulses, nor must we feel exhausted by our efforts to meet our goals. Every time we choose love and ask for the strength and wisdom to overcome temptation, we build our willpower and develop strength within. Even if we find we are unable (or unwilling) to let go of a certain desire, we can ask that our desire for desire itself be lifted. One of the most powerful prayers is for our only desire to be love.

When we detach from specific cravings and outcomes and instead offer all circumstances to love, we draw on its sustaining power and receive the help we need to overcome enticement. It is not an easy road, but it's definitely one we can take steps forward on day by day.

The Hidden Trap

It is important to recognize that one of the greatest temptations we face is to abandon our commitment to love. This manifests in many ways such as disbelief, laziness, lust, and attachment as outlined earlier. We must refuse to succumb to cynicism, doubt, or hopelessness in the face of life's challenges. Love is not a matter of getting what we want; it is a choice we make to satisfy the deep spiritual hunger at the root of all other desires.

Through meditation we develop understanding and awareness, and eventually learn to control the wanderings of the mind. The more we anchor our thoughts in love, the faster we will achieve mastery over the senses and free ourselves from the psychological prison created by desire. Then we will relate to others with as much goodwill and service as we offer ourselves, and our consciousness will dwell in the all-satisfying inner joy of the soul.

A Personal Story

While writing this book, some interesting temptations appeared in my life, giving me the opportunity to personally practice what I hoped to teach here. The biggest temptation of all has simply been to quit: quit writing, quit trying to make a difference, quit trying to love at a deeper level. I have wanted to close the computer and walk away so many times, I lost count. I have wanted to find something less intense to spend my time with, turn off my mind, and close up my heart. It would make life so much (seemingly) easier—to not always be striving for more openness, more understanding, more compassion, and more willingness. But would it really? I have pondered this question and have come to the conclusion that actually, it would not. Once the heart has been opened, it can never fully close again, no matter how much the mind may try to make it do so. The open heart has glimpsed itself as love and wants more, even if the journey is arduous. The soul is relentless in its desire to get home, to reunite with the great love from which it sprang.

When the temptation arose to quit, I remembered that beneath that desire was my soul's longing for freedom—not from the work of loving but of knowing myself and everyone else as the love that we are. I could not and cannot turn away from this.

To overcome the temptation to quit and crawl into a numb ball of non-giving, I have relied upon my daily meditation practice. Whatever I am feeling, I take it to the cushion and offer it to love for transformation. I pray to be replenished with inspiration and become more committed to the process.

Some days, meditation renews me and I feel centered again immediately. Most days, however, it provides only brief respite from my argumentative mind, which kicks back in as soon as I am finished. Cumulatively, however, meditation has brought me the courage and conviction to never ever give up—not on the practice of meditating and not on the practice of loving. Life is one great big test of our willingness to love. Temptation comes and goes, but I will not quit.

Daily Practices

Releasing Desire

Notice the tendency in most situations for the ego to wonder, "What will I get out of it?"

- Practice even-mindedness, even if your personal agenda will not be fulfilled.

- Stay compassionately present and nonreactive, especially in the face of conflict.

- Attempt to be neutral rather than opinionated in most circumstances.

Make Love Your Greatest Desire

Throughout your day check in with these questions.

- What have I thought, said, or done that has taken me closer to love today?

- Am I fostering any habits that take me away from love?

Ask for the strength to overcome desire and to see temptation as training to develop a greater practice of loving.

Willpower Meditation

One of the fastest ways to build self-control and willpower and reduce stress is to adjust your breath rate. At the beginning of your daily meditation, practice slowing your breathing down; you aren't holding the breath, just slowing it down. Start by elongating the exhalation. Then stretch the inhalation. Aim for between four to six breaths per minute. Do this every day for a few minutes before your silent sitting. When temptation arises during the day, employ your slow breathing to get through the impulse reaction.

Chapter Four

....

Anger and Fear: Obstructions to Love

Something amazing happens when we
surrender and just love. We melt into another
world, a realm of power already within us.
The world changes when we change.
Marianne Williamson

As we continue on the path of practicing greater love, the challenges may at times seem daunting. The ever-grasping ego, fighting for its desires, causes us to experience the emotional states of anger when we do not get our way, and fear when we sense scarcity or lack. These two destructive patterns of emotional reactivity—anger and fear—block our experience of love. Great mindfulness is needed to break down these obstacles so we can move forward with a lighter heart.

Root Cause

Consider how upset most of us get when we do not get what we want. Anger is powerful and if left uncontrolled, it can consume us like wildfire. More often than not, anger is fueled by the grasping small self and expressed negatively to defend our position and prove our point. It is an energy that relies upon a self-righteous need to be validated, seen, heard, and given to in the ways we feel we should be.

Underneath all anger seethes thwarted desire. We want things to be different than they are. As a result, resentment festers within us, affecting the quality of our thought, sleep, and productivity, as well as our ability to be in healthy relationships. When we are angry, we behave irritably toward most everyone around us, and this becomes infectious, making others resentful too.

Sometimes we may even *want* the intensity of anger in order to feel more deeply. It can feel good to be indignant or right. There are moments when anger arises that we notice a sense of power that might lead us to be hurtful... or maybe even to *want* to be hurtful. This is the dark side of anger.

On the lighter side, anger can be an activating energy for making positive change. Used wisely, we can learn to transform it through love. To do this, the first thing we must do is to acknowledge the presence of anger but refuse to feed its story or impulses. Instead we can move into compassionate witnessing mode. If we notice that we want to hurt someone because of our anger, we need to look at our belief about how we think things "should" be. This examination will show us how our ego is attached to the situation through desire because again, what triggers anger is usually unmet desire.

Like any emotion, anger is multi-leveled and ever-changing. We must accept all our feelings, positive and negative, and hold compassion for why they sprang into existence. It is unhealthy to disown or suppress feelings, and this is particularly true for anger. If it is held back too long, anger inhibits our ability to see clearly and can easily become a habit as we replay uncomfortable feelings and the story of being wronged or we numb our feelings by escaping into avoidant behaviors. It is equally unhealthy, however, to thoughtlessly spew our anger without regard for its effect. Getting what we want or being right is never worth losing the connection to love in our hearts.

Being able to control the energy of anger is a valuable step toward loving with more intention. The only way we can respond from love is if we do not allow the reactive trigger of anger to fire in our hearts. To prevent this, we need the ability to catch our tongues before they lash out.

What We Feed Grows Stronger

We can practice *being with* anger energetically, observing it rising like a volcano, and remembering that love and inner peace are more important. Then we can withdraw our attention from the anger, allowing it to dissipate through conscious breathing rather than letting it explode. By focusing on the breath, and taking a walk or sitting for a meditation, we control our energy and lessen the power of the angry thought. Rather than asserting outer power, we claim inner power by transmuting the sensory experience of anger through meditation, thereby returning to an openhearted place from which we can respond with love.

Uncontrolled anger is really the ego's useless expenditure of energy. If we can quiet the aggravation of the moment and act *as if* we were feeling love, we will do the right thing. And if we can remember the omnipresence of love, we will feel no obstruction and no lack.

If we hope to channel anger in a way that will not block the flow of love (often for and from the very people who mean the most to us), we must cultivate self-control. This learned skill is an internal muscle built incrementally, day by day through meditation. By limiting our expression of angry thoughts and committing to practices that transform anger into awareness, we begin loving anger out of our systems.

The complete transformation of anger can only come when we want to be free of that energy more than we want to be right, validated, or supported. To do this, we must make our highest desire that which brings us closer to love. We can ask for the gift of grace through prayerful intention: "I no longer want this rage within me." Then we can move beyond strategies of defense and protection into compassion for ourselves and others involved.

Compassion Is Key

Human love relationships have forever been characterized by the dualities this material world is subject to; joy one day, suffering the next; trust then betrayal; selflessness then selfishness; happiness then sadness; passion then burn-out. This is the reason so many people experience similar patterns of disappointment in one relationship after another. If we can see our part in the perpetuation of this cycle, we can be accountable for changing our behavior, owning our experience rather than blaming it on someone else. Then if we are wronged or hurt, we will give voice to our feelings of anger with calm understanding.

The best way out of feeling resentful and unloved is to give more love, and in order to do this we must know love within, which begins with self-compassion. How do we treat ourselves? Are we internally kind and understanding or are we constantly self-critical? We must break down the walls around our hearts to make space for love to breathe.

As we focus on our inner essence rather than our outer struggles and shortcomings, we begin to let go of blame and irritation. We release judgment and replace it with understanding. We trade selfishness for empathy. We open our hearts in compassion and extend love to all beings, remembering that we are one beloved family.

There is no strain in this because there is no ego effort. It is pure peace—the expression of divine love's omnipresence—in contrast to the limitations of the ego's love. We see an example of this great compassion in the masters of all spiritual paths and religions. They hold no expectations of return, no judgments of worth, just a constant changeless stream of love embracing whomever is in their path.

The Shadow of Fear

If we hope to follow in the footsteps of the masters and experience the fullness of love, we must risk looking honestly at the protected places of inner wounding that inevitably appear when we begin to open our hearts. Whatever limits we hold within, we will eventually project into our love connections with others. This is the shadow of fear, which although originally given to us as a survival instinct has been put into hyperdrive in our modern psyche.

So many of us have been betrayed, abandoned or hurt in the past. Now we need to sit with our fear as we would sit with a child frightened of the dark, soothing and comforting ourselves with love until we can see the present clearly again. In this compassionate way, we can recognize the ways in which fear colors how we experience life, limiting us until we bring it into the light of awareness for change.

Additionally, we should examine how the fear of change itself impacts how we live life. Maybe we are afraid to take reasonable risks or are unwilling to embrace the unknown. Maybe we consistently avoid change. Maybe we are battling the natural aging process of the body by obsessing about a youthful appearance. We all cling to our identities as we know them right now and spend too much energy in small self-preservation, fearing that *we* might go away.

Dying Into Self

The fear of death is one of the greatest and most fundamental human fears. This applies to both physical dying and to the death of our created identity. Defined by our bodies, relationship roles, or career titles (all of which are temporary and destined to end), it is easy to fear change. If we only know and value ourselves through external roles and relationships, when we lose them it is a type of death for our egos that can make us doubt our worth or lovability.

If we commune with our souls in meditation, we can learn to live in our bodies without thinking of them as who we *are*. We can break through the delusion of fear (essentially the forgetfulness of our divinity) and come to know the Self that is beyond the physical body. Then we no longer fear the changes that the human vessel goes through in its roles or costumes.

By shifting this identification, we can then embrace change in our lives with more ease because we see that *we* actually remain the same. The essence of who we are still exists regardless of any external circumstance that fluctuates around us. This enables us to release much physical, mental, and emotional pain.

Through meditation we cultivate a positive relationship with our essential nature, allowing it to reveal the ways in which we are blocking love through fear. As the fearful mind quiets and we reconnect with pure awareness within, we practice compassion for our worrisome thoughts without identifying with them. We call out fear in all its hidden forms, not letting it fester in anger, spite, jealousy, or malice.

In later chapters, we will delve more deeply into the passage of physical death and how to navigate it with greater love. For now, suffice it to say that if we allow our energy to be drained by fear, especially fear of the inevitable physical transition of death, we are preventing ourselves from a full and happy life. Knowing others and ourselves *as* love rather than temporal physical bodies helps us to remain peaceful, even when the body passes away. Tuned to the inner Self through meditation, we find an indestructible reservoir of love and beauty, rich in essence although intangible in form.

By dismantling anger and fear, and replacing them with love, we reclaim the totality of our life energy. When these inner obstacles disappear, love flows from our inner being with no limitations, attachments, or expectations of return. Then we embrace life and death as experiences in Self-awareness rather than self-preservation.

A Personal Story

At month five of my second pregnancy after a routine ultrasound, my husband and I were told that our baby would most likely not make it to term. If she did survive, the doctor said, she would be severely handicapped.

I walked out of the doctor's office feeling a combination of fear and anger that I cannot compare to any other experience in my life. On one hand, I did not want to believe the news and was too afraid of what it meant for the future. On the other hand, I felt incredibly angry at being robbed of the joy of pregnancy and the potential of knowing my little girl.

Overwhelmed and unsure as any parents would be, we discussed our options. After some agonizing nights, we decided to carry on with the pregnancy regardless of what might come. I fluctuated daily between trying to be optimistic and inwardly feeling so resentful and sad that I could barely be around my other pregnant friends. I felt envious rather than excited for them and wished that I did not have to bear this dark cloud over the remaining months of my pregnancy. Rather than joyous anticipation, I fought back a growing anxiety. All we could do was pray and prepare ourselves mentally, as best we could, for the possibility of raising a handicapped child.

As the months went along, she did continue to grow and although she was developmentally behind, we were still hopeful that she would make it. I painted a mural on the nursery wall and decorated the room with stars and moons, optimistically *willing* the positive arrival of our daughter. She was not very active in the womb, but I felt a deep connection with her and talked with her daily about how much she was loved and wanted.

As we neared term, we went in for another routine ultrasound. The doctor took a while with the scan and then told us that she could no longer find a heartbeat. In that instant *my* heart stopped beating as well.

There are no clear emotions in these situations, just shock and numbness. And there are really no words. We were given an hour or so to gather ourselves and then were admitted for an induced birth. I could not believe after all the prayer and positive thinking we had held to from month five to month nine and with the resolve to love this child unconditionally regardless of her physical condition, that we would not even have the chance to meet her. Nothing could have prepared me for the anguish of that night.

I was given Pitocin to make labor begin, but knowing full well that on the other side there would be no joy of holding my baby girl, I believe my body did not want to let go. The hours waiting for the drug to kick in was one of the worst times of mental pain I have endured. After hours of slow labor, I finally screamed for relief from my own mind and was given some morphine so I no longer had to feel.

I drifted in and out of awareness for the rest of that night while my body went through the labor process. Early the next morning, I felt a moment of clarity and letting go in my heart. I knew my holding on to the physical form of this child within my womb would not bring her back to life. In that moment, I felt a surge as her body emerged, and then a wave of the most profound sorrow words cannot describe.

They cleaned her body and then the doctor asked if I wanted to hold her. In that moment, the veil of sorrow lifted to a crystal clear thought that I remember as though it was yesterday. "I do not need to see the dead body of my baby. *She* is not in there. She is an eternal soul and she is free."

A photograph was taken in case I changed my mind one day, but in sixteen years I never have. I know as clearly now as I did then that her soul is alive and that I can love her, my Carina Rose, as completely in that way as I could in her physical form. That is her true Self and we are connected in love.

The loss of mothering a daughter remains one of the deepest losses of my life. I could have remained bitter, and I know other mothers who have suffered similar bereavements who have. But I choose to focus on what she taught me instead, unconditional love. Without her nine-month passage through my life, I am not sure I would know what it means to love beyond all personal desire, attachment, and agenda.

We have no control over so many things in life. But we do have power over *how* we love. It is with the most tender gratitude for her that I can say I learned how to love.

Daily Practices

Anger Management

Think of something you have been angry or resentful about for a long time. Notice what is beneath the anger, what desire is unfulfilled? Imagine what it would it feel like if you could let the anger go. Generate the feeling of peace for a moment, just as an experiment. Then if you are ready to be free, drop into your heart and release the unsatisfied desire. Transform it into a higher desire for peace, freedom, or understanding. Practice controlled deep breathing for ten minutes.

Loosening Attachment

Notice the situations in which you feel upset or afraid. How are you attached to the idea of something being different from how it is? Resistance to "what is" keeps us from openhearted loving. What blocks you from being accepting and loving today? Just observe your feeling and recognize that you are enabling your emotional state. Try loosening attachments and opinions. Breathe in love and watch the mind quiet and the heart soften.

Compassion Meditation

Breathe slowly and deeply. Repeat these blessings silently with loving kindness and compassion in your heart.

> May I be free of all obstacles to love in my heart.
> May I be held in love's peaceful embrace.
> May I experience ease in my body, mind, and soul.
> May I feel myself as love.

Next visualize someone you love and send her the same blessings. Continue through people in your larger family, community, and country, and eventually extend the blessings to all beings throughout the world.

Chapter Five

....

The Gift of Vulnerability

If we want greater clarity in our
purpose or deeper or more meaningful
spiritual lives, vulnerability is the path.
Dr. Brené Brown

Going a step deeper now into the shadow of fear, we ask the intimate question, "How could I possibly be known in all my less-than-perfectness and still be worthy of love?"

We all fear the potential rejection that comes with being fully seen. Our egos feel vulnerable when at risk for judgment or criticism, so we hide our inner frailties and strive to present only the strong or positive aspects of self to the world. Yet if we do not challenge the inner critic that strives at every turn to protect our personal identity, we will miss a great reward, the gift of deepening love through vulnerability.

Authentic relationships are forged through the willingness to share the ways in which we do not feel strong or capable, or have made mistakes, and by encouraging others when they share their weaknesses with us. As we practice compassionate self-acceptance, we can allow others to see us in our imperfection. We are relieved of having to make excuses, blame, hide, posture, defend, or hope that someone will think we are different from how we are. When the heart is open, the soul is free. Transparency is wildly liberating.

Vulnerability Practice

We build inner strength by letting go of the belief that we need to be, or even can be perfect, and by *practicing* vulnerability. Love already knows our less than perfect human nature. And it knows that as souls we are so much more creative, resilient, brave, and brilliant than we may now realize. The catch is that in order for love to convert our vulnerability from a weakness into strength, we must embrace our fear of *being* vulnerable. Every moment offers an opportunity to do this.

Through all the thoughts we hold on to, the reactions we give voice to, and the actions we embody, we have the chance to become vulnerable to love. We grow stronger when we choose to live with an open heart, even if the world is not being a friendly place. We grow stronger when we choose to act courageously, even if we are afraid; and we grow when we choose to express love, even if we are faced with potential rejection.

Consider a way in which you feel vulnerable right now. If you shared this with a trusted friend, might it open a door for greater understanding and love within your relationship? One small step at a time, we can allow people that we believe have our best interests at heart to see where we have needs or are not totally self-sufficient. We can speak our truth, even if it is likely to be met with a conflicting viewpoint. We can stay present and open, even when we feel like closing down and hiding from disagreement. We can confide ways in which we feel small or insecure.

Everyone has been wounded, or had her love betrayed in the past. By sharing this vulnerability with those in your life now, you might not *always* be understood, but you will gain the support of those who do. If your experience up until now has been a lack of support or understanding, be discerning of who you choose to share with, but by all means keep trying until you find your tribe of supporters.

The Love–Fear Spectrum

How you feel right now about being vulnerable is a good indicator of where you are on the spectrum of love versus fear. In order to be capable of vulnerability with others, we need to look honestly at our fears while at the same time overcoming self-judgment and fostering self-compassion instead.

So without being critical, simply make a quick mental list of the ways in which you feel fear. What thoughts run through your mind regularly that support those fears? Where did these fearful beliefs originate? Did a family member, respected elder, or religious leader instill them in your thinking?

Begin with this inner witnessing. Assess how fearful beliefs have affected your life and made you feel vulnerable. If there are beliefs you no longer wish to keep, affirm with conviction that you are choosing love as the guiding star of your life now that you realize you have a choice.

Next, make another mental list of all the ways in which you experience love. Then overlay these thoughts of love onto the circumstances and beliefs of fear from the first list. For example, let us say you feel fearful about insufficient finances. The repetitive fearful thought that runs through your mind is "I do not have enough money." But in your love list you notice that you always feel an abundance of love while out in nature. Practice replacing every lack-based thought about finances with a love-centered thought such as, "The infinite creator of nature knows my needs and supplies them each day."

Another example might be that you fear sharing your need for more quality time with your partner. Repetitive thoughts such as "He never listens to me" or "He will not understand my feelings" plague your mind. Yet when contemplating how you feel love, you remember being deeply heard by a friend or teacher in school some time when you were upset. Transfer this energy of loving into a positive thought such as "As I express my vulnerability, I am supported by the energy of love and magnetize to my life those who can meet my needs."

Turning Complaints Into Requests

When we feel afraid that our needs will not be met, it is easy to shrink back and hide or lash out in a way that tries to make someone else responsible. Practicing vulnerability is not a license to push our neediness onto others. We are responsible for our own inner growth and for clear outer communication.

Instead of voicing our vulnerabilities in a way that may be blaming to another, it is far better to let them be heard as direct requests for the love that we need. For example, if you would like your spouse to spend more quality time with you, ask directly for what you want instead of complaining that his working late means he does not love you enough: "One evening a week, I would like us to sit and talk after dinner, with no distractions of work, kids, cell phones, and so on."

Turning complaints into requests honors the fact that there are many ways people feel and express love. These differences do not need to be the source of conflict if we practice vulnerability and use them as opportunities to communicate our needs and feelings lovingly and respectfully. Making a vulnerable request is not judging the other person or his way of doing things as wrong. It is just requesting a change in behavior. "I need you to spend time listening to me without any interruptions" is different than "You are so obsessed with your phone that you can't even put it down to have a conversation with me!"

Criticizing the other person engages a power struggle, but sharing our vulnerable self does not. It simply focuses on finding a solution based on love through patient and respectful communication. Each choice we make in thought, word, and action determines our experience of life. Ultimately, every choice we are faced with comes down to either love or fear.

All Part of the Practice

There are never any guarantees when practicing vulnerability. Sometimes we may ask for a need to be met by another and find that the person is unable or unwilling to do so. Sadly, there will be times when someone may even use our vulnerability against us, and yet even here at the core of painful experience lies a seed of personal growth and strength.

As we offer our vulnerable self to another in full recognition that we may not be met with validation, support, or acceptance, we build courage. Every challenge in front of us is the perfect situation for our evolution in love at this time. All our moment-by-moment decisions to be vulnerable add up to create an inner strength within us that is unshakable.

Ultimately, admitting our deepest longing for love is one of the most vulnerable things we can do; it is essential before our hearts can actually receive it from another. Without the courage to face our own vulnerability, and to share it authentically with others, we will not evolve psychologically or spiritually. On a mental level, we will stay stuck in the places that have made us feel vulnerable to begin with, i.e., our fears and self-doubts. On the spiritual level, we will fail to draw forth our soul's maximum expression and the clarity we need to fully know love. Our self-created wall of protection keeps us from the very thing we long for.

When we think "I am sure to be hurt again if I put myself out there," "I am not worthy of success in love," or "I will never find the relationship that I desire," we are setting up an experience of reality based on fear. And like any other, the fear of being vulnerable limits our life. It is hard to imagine anyone *choosing* a life of limitation, but this is exactly what we are doing when we shrink back and hide our less than perfect parts.

To walk willingly toward that which is difficult takes fortitude. But as soon as we step into courage, even if we are afraid, we generate more power within us. When we decide to think "The Universe is infinite potential, therefore everything I need is available to me now" or "I am made of love, therefore I cannot be separate from it," we create a reality based on love. The more we affirm and pray to know ourselves *as* love, the more we will experience vulnerability as power rather than weakness.

You Are Not Your Story

Letting go of the need to self-protect is an essential step toward living a life of love. When we hold back in efforts to maintain control, what we're really doing is robbing ourselves of potential love. When we get tired of identifying with victimhood and recognize that everyone deeply wants to feel loved and nurtured—yes, even those who have hurt us—we transcend our story of vulnerability altogether. Then we can rest, flow, and play again.

By walking toward challenges with courage and faith and simultaneously releasing attachment to an outcome, we develop an inner security that carries us through the trials of life. The practice of vulnerability makes us more resilient to change and actually less vulnerable over time. In showing up as who we are and accepting our weaknesses and fears with compassion, we open a door for more truthful relationships to flourish and see that we are safe regardless of any outer response.

Never Give Up

Like building muscles through repetitive weight lifting, we build mental muscles of love by choosing it as our focus again and again. Yes, the mind will offer resistance. Just because we can intellectually understand the value of a practice such as this does not mean it will be easy to implement. Mental diligence is required to watch the quality and content of all our thoughts. Discipline is needed to shift negative thoughts into positive ones, and fearful thoughts into loving ones. Do not give up. Choose love as many times as it takes to eradicate fear from your consciousness. Keep acting courageously and lovingly, *even if* you are not feeling brave in the moment.

The more we look beyond the delusion of the ego self to see our true limitless nature as powerful spiritual beings, the braver we become. Realizing that we are part of the one great Self that holds all within it makes the effort to be vulnerable easier because we see that we all share similar fears, insecurities, and needs. Likewise, we are all connected in love.

A Personal Story

The first time I participated in a women's retreat, I had no idea what I was in for. I had been working with a wonderful therapist who was facilitating the weekend intensive and I believed I was ready to go deeper into my healing process. The group that came together was comprised of open-hearted women of a variety of ages all there with the same intent: letting go of old hurt and fear to move into new relationships with a clearer perspective on love.

We started by sharing our stories of the painful experiences that had brought us to therapy and what we hoped to overcome during the retreat. I was impressed with the level of vulnerability and authenticity as each person bared her soul to the group of strangers. Within the first few hours, a sacred circle had formed, built on the foundation of truth and openness.

As the weekend went along, the facilitator took each one of us through a regression exercise, back to the emotionally traumatic experience we hoped to heal so that we could re-experience it from the strength and wisdom of our current selves. Sitting as witness to one another as we each relived excruciating moments of pain further solidified the group as sisters in vulnerability practice. We learned how to ask for what we need in terms of support and to offer it when we could to those who asked.

By the end of the weekend, no one wanted to leave the retreat house or the safety of our loving circle. The facilitator tried to prepare us for reentry into our respective lives by cautioning that we might be transitioning back to people who were not ready to be in the same open space we had been in with one another or to no one at all, both of which were challenges of loneliness after the intense bonding we had shared.

I was in a new relationship at the time, eager to connect with my boyfriend. I believed he would welcome me home with understanding and support. We met for ice cream and I recounted with retreat-level vulnerability what I had been through over the weekend. As I told my story, I could feel further emotions welling up for release. Not often one to ask for help, I decided to practice stepping out of my comfort zone—I asked him to stay with me that night, to hold and comfort me. He said that he could not; he was going through something of his own and was not capable of supporting me at that time. I felt hurt and abandoned in my moment of need, but then I remembered the strength I had cultivated through vulnerability on the retreat.

It was a true lesson in how we get stronger every time we put our authentic self on the line. I had taken a risk in sharing with him, and he too had been authentic in telling me what he could and could not do in that moment. I had to collect myself and go home to hold my own space. In doing so, I learned that I was capable and that it is okay to say no to another, even someone we love, if we cannot offer what they need. As difficult as the moment was, I am grateful that this man inadvertently taught me boundaries of self-honoring and that I was challenged to achieve a new level of inner strength. The experience served me well as I continue to practice vulnerability in all my relationships.

Daily Practices

Courage Exercise

Challenging relationship dynamics offer endless opportunities to grow more courageous spiritually. Reflect on one you are experiencing at this time. Ask yourself:

- What am I supposed to learn from this particular challenge?

- How can I be more vulnerable to love here?

- How can I demonstrate my courage to love?

Vulnerability Practice

Think of a friend or family member who pushes your buttons. To practice the vulnerability of loving without seeking love in return, write a letter to the person, letting them know the things you love about them with no concern that they appreciate or approve of you, or love you back. You can send the letter or not. It is simply meant as an exercise in perspective for you to set aside the things the person does that bother you and just practice loving.

Strengthening Meditation

The breath is the bridge between body and soul, and it is a powerful aid when we feel vulnerable. Deep, rhythmic breathing soothes the parasympathetic nervous system. Focusing on the heart center as we breathe helps us calmly detach from the drama and turmoil life presents. Anytime we feel separate or afraid, we should cling to the tether of love through our breath.

Take notice: Does your heart feel courageous in love, strong and open? Or does it feel fearful of being vulnerable, weak and closed? If it feels afraid or shut down, begin deep and rhythmic breathing. With each breath, imagine you are drawing strength up from the earth beneath you through imaginary roots. Feel love fortifying you and filling your heart, awakening new courage to be more present in your relationships. Continue with this visualization and the deep breathing for five minutes or more.

Chapter Six

·····················

Trust: The Foundation
for Love

*Perhaps everything that frightens us is,
in its deepest essence, something
helpless that wants our love.*
Rainer Marie Rilke

I chose to put the chapter on vulnerability before the one on trust because I believe that it is only by embracing our vulnerability that we *learn* to fully trust. In the same way that thoughts create experiences, our willingness to be vulnerable creates an experience of inner trust. The more we put our authentic selves out there, the more we realize that we can handle whatever comes back. By creating a foundation of trust within, we are able to love more freely.

Some might argue that it is foolhardy to share our vulnerable side until we believe in the trust-*worthiness* of a person or situation. Yet if we look at what it takes to be trustworthy, I doubt any of us would qualify one hundred percent. Consider these synonyms for the word trustworthy: reliable, dependable, accurate, responsible, steady, steadfast, loyal, faithful, honorable, honest, ethical, principled, moral, incorruptible.

"Incorruptible" is the most interesting word in the list. It means perfect and unchanging, and as we know, nothing in the material realm is. Constant change is simply the nature of things, and everyone is fallible. So how can anything or anyone be trustworthy?

Because we know the imperfection of the material world, most of us walk around with an internal untrusting guard up. We assess whether people will do what they say, be there when we need them, and understand us the way we intend. If we believe they will, we extend temporary trust and wait to see if they deliver.

Being Vulnerable to Trust

To open a deeper level of trust within our hearts that is connected to love, we must choose to believe in the inherent goodness of the soul of each person, regardless of their human imperfections. In his book *The Speed of Trust,* Steven Covey explains that by gifting our trust to someone, we actually enable the person to *become* trustworthy. A person's hidden soul qualities are waiting to be brought forward through the extension of our trust and love.

This evolution of trust is easy to see with children. We entrust them with greater responsibilities as they mature, and they evolve their capabilities as a result, earning both our trust and their own self-trust. Likewise, when we entrust our vulnerability to those around us, we enable them to offer back to us their authentic inner selves. In this way, trust based in love is built.

To trust anyone or anything begins simply as a choice between love and fear. As we saw in the last chapter, we must choose which perspective we wish to live from. Fear keeps us in the human and fallible level of consciousness, forgetful of the indomitable and ever-loving soul. But if we create a sanctuary of love within our hearts, we can trust in little and large ways every day.

As we build trust in the inner Source of love—the divine Self of which we are all part—we become able to interact with people of all levels of trust-*worthiness*. Every circumstance we find ourselves in is an opportunity to deepen our reliance upon love, turning inward to find safety regardless of what is happening around us. Whether the person we are relating to is trustworthy or not from a human standpoint, we hold peace in our hearts and use our intuition to discern whether a relationship is safe or desirable. Rather than feeling small, afraid, or out of control, we navigate situations with ease.

Radical Trust

As we make loving our spiritual practice, we move beyond the world's paradigm of who, what, and why we should or should not trust. We decide from our expansive awareness rather than from a place of contraction and skepticism; the more we do this, the more we develop the ability to relax and flow with life. If not, we become armored against tenderness and optimism, living in a battlefield of paranoia. The world is dangerous and unpredictable, *and* we will not change it by withholding trust. By opting in to vulnerability, we begin healing the divides that have been created by our collective dementia regarding love. Taking a radical step in the direction of love—even when it does not make sense on the outside to do so—is an act of bravery.

The Indian peace leader Mahatma Gandhi offers the perfect example of this radical trust through his mission of nonviolent protest. He put his belief in the power of truth and love into action. He acted with compassion and understanding, even with those who stood in opposition to him. When we are committed to trusting love, we can do the same. The inner strength we build from practicing vulnerability enables us to face our fears and limitations without any defense, blame, or judgment.

Our continued practice of meditation increases our intuitive capacities and helps us trust our own ability to distinguish circumstances that could be emotionally or physically dangerous. There will no doubt be times that we will be let down or betrayed, and these are the very moments in which we must make the decision to love anyway. These are the times we practice faith and nonattachment to personal agenda, accepting that being wounded in the fight for love is far better than resting in distrust.

Turning the Trust Mirror Around

If we do not develop the willingness to extend trust, we will be trapped in the negative mindset created by pointing fingers at other people's shortcomings and the failures of the world at large. The absolute *most* effective way to change the quality of the world we live in is by changing the way in which *we* live. So it is helpful to turn the mirror of trust back upon ourselves, to see where we need to be more accountable. By clearly reflecting on our weaknesses and strengths, the ways we succeed, and the ways we fall short, we begin to see how *we* may not be totally trustworthy.

Do you do what you say you are going to do consistently? Are you able to follow through from idea to action? In what ways do you walk your talk, or not? Do you ever break promises?

If you discover places that need work, it is time for self-evaluation. This is not the same as self-judgment, which is harmful. The qualities of self-acceptance and self-trust go hand in hand. We become trustworthy when we can authentically self-reflect and see what we need to change, when we share our truth even if we are met with criticism, and when we act from our highest soul values even in difficult situations. We build self-trust when we honor our feelings rather than deny, project, or rationalize them away. And we strengthen inner trust when we persevere regardless of setbacks and failures. Our own life is the only place we have control, and through consistent behavior and authentic inner reflection we learn to trust ourselves.

Inner Commitments

As long as we identify solely with the ego personality, our self-esteem and self-worth will fluctuate according to how well we perform or how much others validate us, an endlessly swinging pendulum between joy and suffering. But when we shift our identification from small self to soul Self, we remember our completeness in love and realize that we are not separate struggling beings but part and parcel of love. By committing to remember this every day, we develop courage and trust the soul Self to guide the fallible human self.

Our inner commitments help us maintain overarching values in life, ones that inform all the outer movements we make. Unlike goals that define *what* we want to accomplish in life, inner commitments define *why* we do what we do. Think of them as intentions that lead us closer to external goals. Here are some examples:

- Make choices based on love not fear
- Prioritize personal spiritual growth

- Share vulnerability rather than hide in distrust

- Live mindfully, present in each moment

- Know our true spiritual Self

- Live more from soul and less from ego

If we wish to move into a more expansive experience of love, we must define inner commitments for our lives that reflect this dedication. As we stay true to our personal vision for a life of meaning, purpose, and love, we maintain our equanimity regardless of life's inevitable emotional challenges.

Love Builds Trust

As we take more responsibility for our inner world, we come to trust the moment and ourselves in the moment, regardless of life's constantly changing circumstances. We begin to care less about the destination and more about the commitments that guide our way to loving purely and freely. And we become more compassionately responsive to our outer world.

Daily meditation practice helps empty the mind of external forces that weigh on us, cleansing inner perception so we can hear intuitive solutions and guidance. Real trust lives beyond the rational mind. In fact, the mind may not ever fully understand the promptings of trust-led consciousness— and that is okay. The mind cannot fully know love either, but the heart does.

Although it is human nature to cling to things and people we *think* will keep us safe or in charge, anyone who has lost a beloved knows that life will not be controlled. It is here on the field of insecurity that we must learn to master courage by maintaining our practice of vulnerability, trusting that we are safe inside the greater reality of divine love. Fear simply cannot occupy the same space as love. They are like darkness and light. When the light goes on, the darkness disappears. Love will always prevail over fear if we commit to it. Love antidotes hatred, judgment, and prejudice; trust counteracts fear, worry, and doubt. In every moment, it is up to us to choose whether love or fear will guide us. They cannot both run the show.

It Is All About Perspective

One year, I realized the power of electing to trust when I rented a beach house in New Hampshire. Each morning I would sit and meditate in front of a large window facing the sand dunes and the sea. The window's double-pane seal was broken and because of this, moisture created a fog inside the window that I could not clear. Little rivulets of dampness would trickle down and make streaks that distracted me; I thought they were unsightly.

I would often catch myself focusing on the fog and the streaks, an irritating barrier between me and the clear view of the majestic beauty outside. One day, I relaxed my vision and focused on the distance rather than the foreground. Suddenly, the distracting and ugly view disappeared and my vision merged with the brilliant colors and contours of grassy dunes and the rising sun beyond. I perceived the morning's beauty once again. Trust is like this.

As humans in a flawed world, we will forever find reasons why we dare not trust, extend ourselves in vulnerability, or love. From political leaders to partners and friends, people have and will continue to betray us, go against their word, and fail to live in truth. Everything in this world is unpredictable, imperfect, and un-trust-worthy. It is *also* true that we are looking at the fog and the streaks, not the magnificence beyond them.

It is within the quiet inner space of meditation when our egos relax where we can approach the grandeur. Even one moment of pure awareness reveals a love so great that it is beyond measure. No person, however trusted they may be, can give this to us—it is already right there waiting within us. All defenses become unnecessary as we let go into the love that created us.

A Personal Story

When my son was ten years old, he and I were traveling in a remote part of rural Mexico. We had stayed several nights at a small inn and enjoyed chatting over dinner with other guests and the local workers. One day, we were invited to visit and swim in a private cenote, a sacred fresh water sinkhole that ancient Mayans used for ceremony and occasionally sacrifice. Many are overrun with tourists and have lost their sanctity and magic, so to visit a private one was a rare treat. The two men who would take us there spoke only a few words of English, but we were up for the adventure.

The men drove us many miles away from the inn and indicated that we would need to walk into a thick jungle, at which point I began to question their trustworthiness as well as my decision-making as a mother. After trekking for about a mile and a half, we came to the edge of a massive crater in the earth. We gingerly approached the edge to peer down. About 80 feet below was the most crystalline blue water I had ever seen, surrounded by stunning flowering trees and colorful, chirping birds. I asked in broken Spanish how we were to get down to the water for our swim.

One of the men reached into a nearby tree, pulled out a harness, and handed it to my son. Now, this was no safety-inspected American climbing gym harness equipped with carabineers and accompanied by liability waivers. This was a rough-hewn, well-worn, leather contraption with ropes running through it that looked like it had seen better days. These strangers were asking me to strap my son into it so they could lower him down into a cave-like hole in the earth where their ancient ancestors had conducted sacrificial ceremonies. I had only a moment in which to choose: run for our lives back through the unknown jungle, or trust. My young son beamed at me with exhilaration at this Indiana Jones style adventure. My intuition said *go*, so I abandoned all fear, helped him step into the harness, and said, "See you down below." A few moments later, it was my turn to belay myself into the cavern, trusting that our guides would not cut the ropes and leave us there as gifts to the gods.

Once inside the cenote, we swam in the glistening blue lagoon, surrounded by sculptured stalactites. When we tired, we rested on the sandy island in the center and gazed up into light-strewn rock portals draped with ferns and flowering vines. If I had followed my fear, we would have missed one of Earth's paradisiacal gems and an exquisite moment of life. I am so glad trust won my heart and love led the day.

Daily Practices

Clearing the Fog

Take a moment to consider what your personal barriers to trust are … the fog and streaks you habitually focus on that keep you from trusting love completely. Go back to the Ego vs Soul exercise in chapter one, and notice the beliefs you hold about love and why trusting love may be challenging. How might your beliefs be keeping you from seeing beyond to a different perspective? What might change if you stopped looking at the untrustworthiness of the world and concentrated on the inherent trustworthiness of love instead?

Inner Commitments to Love

Are your goals in life driven by fear or love? If you were to trust love more, what might change? Write down three inner commitments or pledges to the overarching values you hold around love.

Trust Meditation

If you have not already, begin a daily meditation practice. Even ten minutes a day practiced consistently will make a huge difference in your ability to feel conscious trust. When you are still, watch the ways in which the ego mind distrusts but the soul is just fine and feels peace no matter what. Compassionately recognize the feelings that try to hang you up, but keep expanding even more into love.

Chapter Seven

....

Allow Yourself to Be Loved

"We are not held back by the love
we didn't receive in the past, but by
the love we're not extending in the present."
Marianne Williamson

In the same way that we will never be 100 percent trust *worthy* in our fallible human nature, we can never be completely love *worthy* either, regardless of how hard we try. The good news is that we do not have to be. We do not need to earn love because it is who we *are*.

Given this truth, imagine what it would be like to be *totally* loved and *totally* accepted exactly as you are right now, not because you acted as someone else wanted you to or did something to care for them, but just because you are sitting here reading and breathing. Really try to imagine what pure love and acceptance would feel like.

Most of us have a hard time shifting our perception on this topic because we still relate to love in its human conditional form and do not yet know ourselves *as* love. When we feel separate and defined by our human stories, we live in a perpetual lack of love, always sensing our inadequacy. When we do not feel loved or lovable, it is because we have fallen back into a belief of disconnection. Sadly, we reinforce this belief of lack in our relationships, becoming disillusioned quickly with the other person's inadequacies as well.

As long as we define our love-worthiness by our ego's beliefs about who we are, we will be unhappy. And trying to become more self-loving, from a psychological standpoint, will never bring us fulfillment because these efforts only feed bits of temporary solace to the already-desperate ego.

It is only when we move beyond our limited, personal self to find connection with the greater Self, remembering that love is always shining through us, to us, around us, and within us, that we overcome the beliefs of lack and separation. When we recognize the same consciousness in the person sitting across from us as we do within ourselves, we cannot help but feel connected. We are all animated by the same life force energy and the same love; it is simply filtered by our personalities.

Preparing the Heart

In the same way that we cannot capture a gallon of rainwater in a tiny cup, our experience of love is limited by the size and quality of the vessel through which we receive, i.e., our hearts.

To be able to hold the vast love that awaits us when we find our way home to the recognition of true Self, we must prepare ourselves. This is a multi-step process.

As we have been doing, we gently examine our human personality and all the dramas it has endured and created. We recognize that the small self *is* the drama. We maintain compassion for its journey because being human is not easy. At the same time, we remember that in our true essence, we are not broken beings defined by stories of shame, sorrow, and failure. We only think we are because we have been living with a false perception of ourselves, one that makes us believe in limitations and worthlessness.

The longer we see ourselves incorrectly, the more we will repeat our self-created suffering in our own minds and relationships. As the saying goes, insanity is doing the same thing over and over and expecting a different outcome. To change this game, there are four mental attitudes necessary to purify and prepare our hearts: kindness, compassion, honor, and equanimity.

Kindness dawns as soon as we accept that we are not separate from any other being; we recognize that anything we do to another we do in some way to ourselves. If we are one with all other beings, how could we possibly indulge envy or hatred?

Moving deeper into this awareness, we begin to suffer with all those still in the delusion of not knowing who they truly are, feeling the pain and fear that comes with that level of consciousness. As a result, our compassion grows.

With more practice of conscious loving, we elevate others and ourselves to our rightful divine status. We act with respect and honor toward everyone. Day by day, we patiently wade through the ongoing trials of the small self, struggling in imperfect experiences of lesser love. In doing so, we learn equanimity. Eventually, our awakened heart reclaims its spiritual birthright as unconditional love.

More Than a Feeling

Any separation or loss we feel is really the soul grieving its perceived separation from love. Although limitation is experienced when the soul comes into a physical body, it is ever-expansive by nature, which is what the practice of meditation reconnects us with—our limitlessness beyond the drama of human experience. As soon as we realize that we are still connected to the divine energy of love, the feelings of sorrow and loss lessen measurably.

Our daily task is to catch the thoughts of separation that discourage us and make us feel unworthy and instead come back time and again through our meditations to the love within. Granted, we may not always *feel* loving, but healing and reconnection begin when we imagine, "How would I act if I knew that I *am* love?" Acting as if we know that we are love opens the door of our heart by generating compassion, kindness, patience, humility, acceptance, and non-judgment. This is not accomplished through fake smiles or niceties but by reaching beyond the emotional lack of a particular moment and acting from a more conscious place within.

We have the choice to *act* lovingly, to be compassionately present to the one in front of us. When we do, we immediately feel the love we were seeking. Take a moment and notice how you would act if you actually felt love right now.

No Limits to Love

Opening ourselves in this way, we see that love can express itself in infinite ways. If there is a specific way in which we deeply want to feel loved, we can call out to the Source of all love, asking to feel it in our hearts in that specific way. Maybe we need a nurturing love or a protective love, a wise guiding love or a faithful friend love. The aspect of love we want to feel already lives within us and waits to be drawn forth. Consider how you would most like to feel love, and trust that it will reveal itself to you in just that way.

To commune with the divine Source of love, we must practice seeing it all around us, in all that is here and now. If we appreciate the beautiful flowers in our garden, we can recognize that love is manifesting in those flowers and shining back at us through their radiant faces. The joy we feel with our pets is love expressing itself to us in those unique forms. Our friends and family are all reflections of Source love offering us reminders that we are not alone or separate. This is a beautiful way to meditate on love and open new personal experiences of divine connection.

Relax Into Receiving

Because our well-being depends on our ability to give and receive love completely, it is time to release any and all beliefs that limit love. Receiving is an acquired skill just as giving is, and we need to become unconditionally receptive to love in all its forms.

Sometimes we block it as it comes to us from another because the way they choose to express it is not necessarily the way in which we most wish to receive it. For instance, someone may be capable of expressing love through a kind gesture but not through clear communication. If we can release judgment and allow ourselves to receive love as it is given, we will feel an expansion. If we limit love to the ways in which it feels most comfortable or familiar to us, we may miss many opportunities to receive it.

Part of allowing ourselves to be loved is opening up to receive in ways we may not have experienced before. We must also be willing to offer love to another in a way that may feel unnatural to us but meaningful to that person. Every time we expand our ability to receive love, we simultaneously expand our ability to give love and vice versa.

If our intention is to know ourselves *as* love, then any relationship in which we act lovingly will be fulfilling because intention creates meaning. If not, it does not matter how much attractiveness or compatibility might be present at first; love will fade over time. The happiest relationships are those we relate to from our highest Self and that foster our spiritual growth in this life.

Remember that we do not have to *earn* love. Love is always within us and around us, ours from our first breath. As we enlarge and clarify our consciousness, love emerges in new ways and shines through the barriers erected by our personal histories.

Anytime we are not aligned with love, we will notice tension in the mind, body, or heart. Muscular relaxation and mental surrender go hand in hand, and love is the greatest catalyst. As we still the restless mind through relaxation techniques and meditation, we create a receptive field within our beings to fully receive love. This improves our health, energy, mental clarity, and relationships. It diminishes pain, reactivity, fatigue, and fear.

To speak of love intellectually is not enough—we must drop into the quiet space of meditation, cultivate a relaxed stillness within our hearts, and allow ourselves to feel that loving and being loved are actually one and the same.

A Personal Story

I once knew a woman who was a consummate giver. She gave to everyone all the time—little things like rides to work or a plate of cookies as well as big things like houses to stay in and cars to borrow. Yet when anyone tried to give her something, she would immediately push it away and dismiss it completely. She could not take compliments or even tolerate simple appreciation. Even from those she was closest to, she seemed completely unable to receive.

As I got to know her better, I realized that she sought to please others in an attempt to assuage her deep lack of self-worth. Other people's appreciation of her gifts filled her to a degree, but at the end of the day, she would always come up empty because she could not receive true love; it would bounce off her like a penny on a tight sheet. She simply could not absorb the love of another because she did not love herself, and it made me sad. I suggested she try to receive in little ways, like pausing to actually feel it when someone thanked her or paid her a compliment. When I looked into her eyes, I tried to convey that my friendship was not flowing to her *because* she had done something for me but because I genuinely cared about her.

Little by little, the woman began to receive, and I felt a softer openness in our connection where before there had been a hard wall of defense. Over time I watched her start to give to others from a more authentic expression of her goodwill rather than in a search for attention or approval. I was pleased to see her become genuinely happier as a result.

Daily Practices

Mantra Walking
Choose an affirmation from appendix 3 that affirms what you need most from love right now. Take a slow and mindful walk, repeating it with each step.

Exercise to Feel Love

Quiet the mind and tune in to your heart. Imagine there is a filter there, a love filter than enables only love to enter or exit. Generate a stronger and stronger feeling of love. Meet anything that disrupts your inner peacefulness with kindness, compassion, honor, and equanimity. Remember that your real Self is always anchored in love, and perceive love beaming at you through innumerable sources all around in your life. Put more emphasis on calmness and nonreactivity throughout your day, and watch emotional sensitivity and conflict dissolve with greater ease.

Meditation on Receiving

Take a deep breath and release it fully. Allow your shoulders to relax. Let tension drain from your face, your belly, and your neck. Scan the body for any other place that may be holding stress, and gratefully notice any places that feel light and free. Simply witness yourself in this moment with kindness and compassion. Now drop your awareness back a bit so the senses fade into the background and your view rests within. Imagine that you are a large container receiving love. See this container expanding more and more to take in more love. Visualize love expanding within you and around you until there are no boundaries left, just love.

Chapter Eight

....

Overcoming Pain and Insecurity

Your love must be greater than your pain.
Paramahansa Yogananda

Almost every day, life delivers some measure of discomfort or pain. We feel scared in our jobs. We get hurt in our relationships. We lose a desired opportunity. We become depressed because life is not turning out how we hoped it would. Whatever it may be, it is clear that the world will never be able to give us the security we long for, and this is especially true when it comes to human love. The level of love exchanged from one small self to another inevitably changes or falls short of what we need, and we suffer. To depend completely on personal love sets us up for disappointment and an ongoing experience of insecurity.

The only truly safe haven in life is an inward connection to absolute love. To get to this, we need to use each challenge of human relationship as an opportunity to create a deeper connection to Source. We can use all experiences (even hurtful ones) as stepping stones on our journey of remembering that our highest nature *is* love.

Even if someone treats us in a less than kind way—projecting fear, blame, or hatred in our direction—we can use that energy for the development of stronger love within ourselves. We can remember that we are only ever dealing with the singular energy called love manifesting in varying forms, and thus we can acknowledge the spark of Source within every other person. All interpersonal relationships are actually the great Self dealing with itself. So how we choose to relate to each other is a reflection of how we relate to love. Equally true if said in reverse, how we relate to the energy of love determines how secure we will feel in all our human relationships. Like the quote at the beginning of this chapter states, we must grow love within our hearts that is greater than any pain. If we do this, conflict and loss will no longer threaten our self-image or sense of security.

The Love Gap

It takes courage and strength to admit our own shortcomings and to discern where *we* are limiting love. The overarching themes and patterns we experience in relationships with others will show us where we are stuck in our relationship with divine love. This is a profound realization that can lift us from limitation and frustration to freedom in a very short period of time.

If we can summarize in a few words what we are struggling with in human relationships, we can see where the love gap is in our heart. Remember that our human relationships reflect our attitude toward love, and our attitudes about divine love condition our human relationships. The following list offers examples of beliefs we hold in human relationships that parallel how we may struggle to relate to Source love.

- I do not fully trust

- I do not believe my needs will be met

- I do not feel worthy

- I do not really expect response

- I am waiting for material proof in order to believe

- I fear being judged and worry that if I am totally myself, I will not be loved

- I do not feel safe

- I do not believe you care about my suffering

Did you connect with one or more of the above? Consider how you currently experience difficulty in relationships or have in the past. For example, if you are not totally trusting of people, you may have a trust issue with love itself. If you are not completely devoted or people are not devoted to you, you may need to increase devotion to your spiritual practice of loving. If you find that people do not want to spend much time with you, notice how much time you spend with your divine Self. Are you constantly frustrated or dissatisfied with the love of others? Maybe you need to increase your own efforts in practicing love. If you do not feel appreciated, maybe you are not appreciating the blessings of love in your life enough.

When we feel held back in some way from a full relationship with love, we suffer in our own minds and hearts, as well as in our relationships. If we want to improve our human love connections, we can start by deepening our bond with Source love. How do you want to treat love? And how do you want it to respond to you?

The Answer Lies Within

Our human relationships are the practice ground to develop a deeper and more unconditional connection to pure love. We must watch the moments in which the impulse arises to shut down, wall off, or withdraw our love from a person or situation. If conflict arises, rather than condemn the other person, we can reflect on how well we are loving him. If we honestly feel that our heart is clear and open, then our challenge is to remain compassionate and kind to the other person and tend to our own hurt feelings. We cannot stop others from behaving badly, but we can create inner security in love by never retaliating.

It takes an act of strong will to stay open-hearted and connected to love in moments of wounding, anger, or fear. Of course we need to be self-honoring and set appropriate boundaries so as not to be mistreated. But in most cases, the deeper practice is to mindfully watch the fluctuation of our hearts opening and closing. If we feel unwanted, unseen, or unloved, we must initiate the experience of connection we desire from within by connecting back to the pure energy of love itself. Then we can decide on the right outer action. This might look like remaining present during an argument when our impulse is to withdraw and self-protect. It might mean taking extra time to communicate through to a place of understanding, even when we are tired and just want to go to sleep.

Making our love greater than our pain means choosing peace *even if* people misunderstand us, judge us, or criticize us. When we learn to honor and serve all beings as extensions of Self, we see that giving and receiving is just love helping love. If we recognize that life is challenging for everyone, we can be more empathetic and strive to see the soul within every face, regardless of what the person is presenting outwardly. As we become givers of peace, compassion, and understanding, we will actually see more good in others and will be able to draw more goodness from them.

Recalibrating the Heart

The daily practice of conscious loving counteracts the stress we feel from the negativity, selfishness, and self-righteousness in the world around us. Our bodies are affected by all powerful emotions, for better or worse. Benevolent ones like kindness, empathy, and gratitude feel good and are good for us. They help our bodies function optimally. Unloving ones like rage, envy, or fear contribute to stress and tension in the body as well as the mind.

The Institute of HeartMath is a nonprofit organization that conducts research into heart-brain interactions and heart-rate variability with the goal of helping people reduce stress. Their studies show that as the heart valves open and close in continuous rhythm, an electromagnetic field is produced that exchanges energy with other fields around it. This field is altered as we experience different feelings, and it vibrationally impacts every cell in our bodies. A common way to relate to this phenomena is through the experience of feeling grief as heaviness in the heart region.

There is a connection between the physiological function of the heart and the emotional and spiritual feelings we have. When the heart's electromagnetic field is coherent and balanced, our outer relationships are more peaceful. A loving heart creates a dominant rhythm of positivity and peace that sustains and regenerates our energy. This integrated state of being makes us feel secure. But if we are in a state of disharmony, exhibiting feelings such as anxiety and anger, these negatively affect our nervous system and our energy, perpetuating experiences such as shame, blame, and conflict.

We can uplift ourselves by focusing intentionally on love, watching inspiring movies rather than violent ones, reading sacred texts or positive quotations instead of hate-filled news, and listening to soul-filled songs rather than demeaning ones. We can refuel by spending time in nature and honoring the sacredness of life. We can connect with people who are authentic and compassionate, striving for lives of integrity, and we can bless everyone we see by silently acknowledging the divine within them.

When we fall out of balance, we can recalibrate by offering compassion, empathy, and understanding to those around us, focusing on qualities that bring us into a state of integration such as gratitude, peace, and forgiveness. If we are feeling down, the best thing we can do is something for someone else, because this will activate the altruism of our souls and make us happier as a result. By maintaining a loving approach to life and meditating more deeply, we attune our heart rhythms and move from an experience of pain to harmonious connectedness and inner security.

Resetting through Meditation

Our daily meditation practice anchors us in love so that when difficulty arises, we can rebalance more quickly. We look upon each challenge as just another test of our ability to remain in a highly loving place, there to help us overcome reactivity and develop a clearer heart.

We develop the ability to calmly withstand whatever life delivers because we know love as more than just personal emotion; rather it is the essence of our being. Through stillness and concentration, we develop receptivity to love, and from there we sense the right course of action for our lives. With an open heart, we live fearlessly, loving all beings as expressions of the one love.

Meditation makes us peaceful and it eventually teaches us the greatest thing we can possibly learn, which is to be in love with the one pure love. Here we find all that we need, regardless of who is with us in our lives. When we reconnect to love within, we find the truth to solve every problem and the strength to do so. This is the security of love that enables us to overcome all pain.

A Personal Story

Many years ago, I was feeling discouraged in my primary relationship and unsupported as a parent. As a single mom of an eight-year-old boy, I often felt overwhelmed. A mounting sense of isolation from Source was present in my heart, and I had fallen away from daily prayer. Formal meditation was not yet a practice I understood, but I liked to sit and breathe and chant devotional songs sometimes, especially if I was sad or upset.

One morning was especially challenging and I had gone to my yoga studio to get centered before teaching the first morning class. I put on a chant by Krishna Das, a devotional singer I often turned to in order to open my heart when I was feeling oppressed or down. It was early and no one else was in the offices next door, so I cranked the music up and sang at full volume, repeating the chant many times until I had pushed the self-pitying thoughts out of my head. I asked to feel love's support and to understand what inner wall I needed to tear down to relax more into my ability to love. Then I sat in silence.

Suddenly, a profound wave of love washed over me and through me and around me in such a way that I felt engulfed, filled, and buoyed up beyond my capacity to hold it or by any means understand it. It was intense and immense, and tears of joy and ecstasy begun to flow from my eyes, dissociated from any thought of an external person, place, or thing. This went on for at least five minutes … five minutes of unadulterated bliss.

The event was more than a decade ago, but I can feel it as though it just occurred if I tune my heart in, because these moments of opening to love change us forever.

Though meditation is a regular practice for me, I will tell you: these ecstatic moments definitely do not show up daily. They are gifts of grace directly from love, little beacons of light that encourage us on the path. We cannot seek after them, for they will become even more elusive if we do. But they do come when we identify the disconnect with love that keeps us in our pain and surrender it completely. Love waits for us to drop to our knees in supplication, only to lift us again in strength. I treasure that moment to this day and return to the memory of it when I need to recalibrate my heart back to its safe haven of love.

Daily Practices

Discover Your Love Gap

Consider these attitudes that might be lingering hindrances to your full availability to love. When you find the one that is keeping your heart closed, replace it with the affirmation "I *am* love." See how different this feels.

- I do not fully trust love (I am love)

- I do not think my needs will be met in love (I am love)

- I do not feel worthy of love (I am love)

- I do not really expect to be loved (I am love)

- I am waiting for material proof in order to believe in love (I am love)

- I do not feel safe in love (I am love)

- I fear being judged, and worry that if I am totally myself, I will not be loved (I am love)

- I do not believe love cares about my suffering (I am love)

Medicate With Love

Practicing love and compassion stabilizes the heart and balances brain functioning. Try this experiment next time you feel low. Think of a person you feel neutrally about. Send them a thought of compassion. Then think of someone closer to you and send them peace. Keep going through various people in your life, sending the feelings of empathy, generosity, and gratitude. End with the closest person to you and surround them in love. Notice how you feel. Then simply sit with the feeling of love in your heart and notice if an inner bubbling of joy arises. Stripped of the ego's occlusions, the soul radiates its essential nature, which is joy. Love lights the joy spark again within us.

Love Meditation

Breathe slowly and allow yourself to settle into a quiet place. Notice the contents of your mind and heart. Focus your attention at your heart center and breathe in love. Feel yourself sitting inside love itself, no separation. If pain is present, just allow it to be there but visualize love getting more and more intense around you and within you. Breathe love in. Breathe love out. Feel your connection to love becoming bigger and bigger, transforming any element of pain or insecurity.

Chapter Nine

....

Forgiving to Be Free

*You can change the past when
you change the way you see it.*

Alan Cohen

Mistakes are a necessary part of life. Intentionally or unintentionally, we have all wronged others or been unloving at times. To recognize this does not mean that we should be self-condemning. It means that we are ready to acknowledge the ways in which we have failed to love, even if we did not mean to do so, and strive to grow as a result.

If we treat mistakes as feedback to learn from, then our past becomes a valuable resource, a well of information and inspiration for living into the future. Although we cannot change what has already happened, we can change our thoughts about it. In doing so, we change our experience in this moment and of the future that we are creating. If however we remain mired in the agony of remorse, not only have we done damage in the past but we ruin the present moment as well. By accepting full accountability for our thoughts, words, and actions and learning the necessary lessons from the past, we free ourselves to move forward toward greater love.

Which Way Do You Want to Go?

Each moment offers the possibility to draw closer to love, to be indifferent to it, or to move away from it. If we look at every decision and every communication through this perspective, we reduce many of life's complexities and save ourselves much aggravation.

Spending time judging and criticizing ourselves or those around us is not drawing us closer to love. If instead of finding fault we strive to encourage through kindness, we infuse our hearts with compassion and other people's lives with inspiration. If instead of fighting for our point of view we practice patience and acceptance of our differences, we develop emotional maturity and gentler relationships. Love is the way to reach people, to change people. Committed to what moves us closer to love, we build bridges of peace and create more ease in our lives.

Will Versus Karma

Like Newton's law of action and reaction, every thought, word, and deed we have put into the world has an equal response that registers an effect on our lives, for better or for worse. This is the law of karma; according to the teachings of reincarnation, karma carries over from multiple lifetimes. Actions in this particular lifetime may or may not affect consequences that are readily identifiable but they are registered on the grand karmic scale that weighs the balance of our selfish and selfless actions.

According to spiritual master Paramahansa Yogananda, much of both the success and the suffering we experience now are due to actions taken in some distant past, explaining the apparent inequalities in the world around us. Through the karmic principle of spiritual evolution, every person shapes their destiny through thought and action, moving through greater and greater selflessness toward final liberation in pure love.

Whether we choose to believe in reincarnation or not, the effect of karma can be seen in the simple fact that everything we do has some type of consequence. If we eat or drink too much, we feel lousy later. If we rob someone, we may not be stolen from in return, but our peace of mind is altered. If we lie or betray, we may not suffer a similar transgression but will have broken our own internal trustworthiness. All our actions set up future experiences outwardly *and* inwardly. Using conscious will to think, speak, and act from love helps us to create a future of joy and freedom.

Karmic tests help us grow spiritually if we let them. They point out the places we need to open our hearts and become more loving humans. Mistakes become fertilizer for new understanding and the impetus to make necessary amends. A period of daily self-reflection can help us see the ways we may have been hurtful to others and how we can become more caring and compassionate now. By choosing to be accountable for our thoughts, words, and actions today as well as in the past, we can clear any negative karma and secure a happier future.

Acknowledging Trauma

What if someone has deeply harmed or wronged us? How can we make peace with karmic interplay? Before we can answer these questions, it is essential to acknowledge our experiences of pain, loss, victimization, disease, and to *fully feel* all the emotions associated with them. It does not serve our journey toward peace and love to avoid or repress feelings associated with past experiences. Once an emotion has occurred, we cannot deny it or avoid it forever. It will continue to affect our present behavior until we feel emotionally complete. By the same measure, getting stuck in emotions or righteously over-expressing them also sucks energy away from our lives now. There is a balance point between the two.

The key to that balance is to accept our feelings and express them appropriately. We do not need to rationalize them or prove we are right; we only need to take accountability for them without judging, blaming, denying, or defending. We do not need to identify with old experiences or old feelings as who we *are*. We can return to the knowing that *we are love*. In this way, we end the struggle against what is and what has been, and move closer to freedom.

As we recognize the lessons we have learned through painful past experiences, we bring our energy and focus fully into the present. We stop indulging our egos in their fight to be right or pitying them in a story of victimization; we celebrate our souls as they create meaning and become open to resolution. Healing occurs as we release our energetic and emotional cords from the past, recognizing that whatever karma we have lived through has offered a learning ground for our evolution into love. Acceptance allows us to find inner peace and power.

It is never too late to accept, but it can feel like a drastic leap into the unknown. Fear inevitably arises when we start to shed the story that we have told about who we are. We feel unsure, doubtful that we will reach the other side of such a transition. So often we stop the journey, repress the feelings again, and settle down into the familiar zone, even if it causes us pain. At least we know this particular pain—it has been with us for a while, after all. Unfortunately, if we settle for long enough, our souls wither from our awareness. We must allow love to fuel our courage to keep going.

Daily meditation helps us forge forward through any difficulty or change. Each time we sit as witness to our experience, we can see that we are more than it is, in any given moment. As we venture onto the unknown path, and stop struggling against what is, we move out of comfort zones and onto edges of personal growth. We open our hearts to whatever is in front of us, and act from the love that is within. We embrace periods of intense learning as occasions for eradicating non-loving beliefs and behaviors. Regardless of the challenge we are faced with, we strive to open our consciousness wider, and to move deeper into love.

Clearing Karma

"Clearing" does not mean eliminating all pain from our lives—there is a certain amount of karma we have to live through as we clarify our consciousness in any lifetime. The law of karma is neutral and simply a way to look at whatever difficulties we are experiencing as opportunities to develop greater selflessness and Self-awareness. We do not have to define ourselves by anything in the past. If we allow our wounds to become the foundation of our strength and purpose, we open to love now.

Additionally, meditation helps us lessen the effects of karma. Through focused, devotional meditation, we establish peace in our hearts and uplift our consciousness by concentrating on love. We rise above the subconscious mind, where the latent selfish tendencies and temptations live that contribute to, and sustain karmic patterns. In meditation, we tap the super consciousness instead and are inspired toward good actions, forgiveness, and the light of higher awareness. Even if someone has hurt us, we can choose to respond with forgiveness. Nothing is so important that it should make us close our hearts or act selfishly—if we do, we only create more karma for ourselves.

Love Your Neighbor

All negativity and hurtfulness come from deep-seated fear and insecurity that are based in a lack of love. Recognizing this, we can have compassion for ourselves when we fall into them and for others who act wrongfully as well. Often, people who behave unkindly have been denied a healthy experience of love from their family of origin, and so their longing for love has been perverted in unhealthy ways. Their own suffering is often greater than what they inflict on others. We cannot help them through condemnation, only love. Meditation helps us let go of resentment and respond from a higher perspective.

In addition to the use of our free will for goodness and the practice of meditation to elevate our consciousness, prayer is another dynamic way to clear karma. We can pray for release from our karmic patterns. We can pray for those who have hurt us, not just that they be resolved with us, but that they too be aligned with love. We can pray that they be cleared of their difficult karma as well. This is the highest way to heal the wounds we hold from those who have hurt us. Just imagine all old hurt, resentment, or guilt dissolving into love. Would that not be life changing?

We can absolutely change at any moment by choosing love. We are stronger than any difficulty because we are love incarnate. We can train our minds to focus on soul qualities of harmony, generosity, and integrity rather than indulging resentment, rage or ill will. Then the infinite power within us will spring forth and banish any thoughts of pain or victimization.

The Necessity of Forgiveness

To accomplish the above, the one action that helps most is forgiveness. If we want to be free and live a life defined by love, we must forgive those who have hurt us. And, we must forgive ourselves for mistakes made when we knew no better. Finally, we must forgive life itself for delivering so many challenges and not giving us everything we desire.

Lack of forgiveness traps our energy in the past and keeps us stuck in the damaging feelings of blame, remorse, and shame. Holding onto anger only lowers our consciousness and moves us away from love. When forgiveness and compassion take the place of anger or self-condemnation, we can take clear action on things we wish to be different in order to create peace.

We initiate this shift by making love our sole focus, clearing out any space in our minds or hearts that is occupied by vengeful, shameful, or regretful thoughts or feelings. Even if we do not know *how* to forgive in this moment, we can be *willing* to try. By opening ourselves to the possibility, we liberate our hearts and create an opening for new relationships to grow, especially our new relationship with love.

Key to Freedom

Forgiveness is our key to freedom. We are liberated in the instant that we want peace more than we want to justify our pain. Our pardon of our own or another's mistakes is an action taken by our soul for its own benefit.

We do not have to make the leap from unforgiving directly to love. If we have given ourselves permission to feel our feelings as discussed above, but we no longer want to be held hostage by them, then we can be grateful for the opportunity to learn to love bigger than we previously have. When we no longer want to feel hate or resentment for another, and are willing to move to a place of neutrality within our minds and hearts, then we can dive deeper into communion with love in our meditations. In doing so we will be guided from the place of neutrality into a peaceful compassion for the other soul.

To be clear, forgiveness does not mean condoning bad or harmful actions. We are not forgiving the action, just the actor. We create a separation between the person and the behavior, the doer and the deed.

If someone operating from a consciousness that was not based in love has hurt us, we can recognize that they are ignorant of their own true nature—otherwise, they would not have acted so. We can pray that the person be guided by love and that their consciousness be awakened to good. At the same time, we can maintain appropriate boundaries if they are not safe to be around. By praying for and visualizing love for others, we create our own spiritual defense. Then we can love their souls from a distance.

If we are working on forgiving *ourselves* for a transgression of the past that we feel truly sorry for, we can recognize that we acted from the consciousness level we had at that time. Now that we are centered in love and see a better way, we will choose this from now on. With the lesson learned, we can let go.

The Challenge of Forgiving

At times, forgiveness feels all but impossible. Usually this is because subconsciously we believe that by holding ourselves or someone else accountable through a *lack* of forgiveness, we will somehow prevent whatever it was from happening again. The forgiveness inquiry in the exercises at the end of this chapter will help you sort out why forgiveness may feel difficult.

If we hold onto memories and feelings of past hurt, fear, anger, betrayal, et cetera, we will actually attract these same experiences again. Wounds that are not cleaned through the power of forgiveness fester and do not heal completely. But those to which we apply the balm of forgiveness make us stronger and free our lives.

Every world religion teaches forgiveness under any and all circumstance, because through forgiveness, we establish peace within our hearts. As a result, less controversy will affect our lives. It is essential for our journey forward that we focus on the sincere actions of others, not the negatives. No matter how anyone treats us, we must go on giving him love. We are not here to reform others, only to change ourselves.

If we feel inadequate against the challenge of forgiveness or in too much pain to try, we should just keep focus on deepening the relationship with love inside our own being. As we attune ourselves to love, the desire and the strength to forgive will come. Over time, this practice will shift us from a pain-centered consciousness of victimhood to a love-centered consciousness of power. Limitless love is the greatest healing force in the world and the only way to achieve lasting happiness. Never ever close your heart.

A Personal Story

There is no doubt in my mind that we are meant to learn and grow through the difficult things in our lives, but because this is uncomfortable, we often resist the challenge and stay in victim mode. However, life is a relentless teacher and will continue to deliver its message in new ways until we receive it.

This process of repeating similar experiences in different forms has been compared to circling down a screw. We loop around a particular issue multiple times, hopefully in smaller or less intense ways until we have extracted the full and final lesson on that particular topic. When we finally get what we need to learn, we metaphorically fall off the tip of the screw and no longer feel an emotional response when confronted with a comparable situation or person. If we do feel an energetic charge, it is a sure sign we still have something to learn. Often this is a lesson about offering forgiveness to ourselves or to another.

Recently, I was preparing for a meeting with a man with whom I had been in a relationship many years before. I was surprised by a surge of anger that welled up inside me and wondered, "After all the time that has passed and all the therapy I have done, what do I still need to learn?" I thought I had forgiven him and was completely done with things, but my emotional response signaled otherwise.

It took a few days of thrashing about in blame and negative memories before I finally realized that although I had forgiven him, I had not yet forgiven *myself*. I was angry with myself for having accepted so much less than I deserved in this particular relationship. I had allowed myself to feel betrayed, unsupported, and mentally exhausted. I had also diminished my self-worth because of his assessment of me rather than uphold my own conviction of strength. Yet when the relationship ended, I bypassed the necessary process of self-forgiveness by focusing on forgiving him, instead telling myself that I should have no regrets. Clearly, I still had another circle on the screw to complete.

I began praying for all karma between us to be fully and finally resolved. I did not want to feel this anger and self-criticism in my mind, body, or soul anymore. What I wanted more was freedom.

Upon further reflection, I realized that it is impossible to evolve emotionally, mentally, and spiritually and not look back on choices made in earlier years without some measure of dismay. I would not make the same choices today I made a decade prior because they were based on a totally different level of awareness. Now, I did not need to *regret* those choices as much as I needed to *forgive* them. To do this, I thought about what had led me to make the choices I did.

Recognizing that we all default to our place of greatest need, I could see that I had needed the emotional support he provided more than I needed to assert myself in other ways. By acknowledging this, I became reacquainted with a tender place in my heart and offered myself newfound compassion and more love instead of the old self-judgment.

Equally important was determining what I had learned through the relationship. It was time to be free...and not repeat this lesson! As a result of our dynamic, I had grown to value myself more now than in years past. I had learned how important it is to hold my power and walk away if my needs are not being met in any relationship, personal or professional.

With these lessons in clear view and a greater level of self-empathy in place, I forgave myself for not being strong or clear enough to end it sooner. I forgave myself for having emotional needs that made me stay even when I knew it was not right. We had both done the best we could. To hold onto anything other than love now would just keep me imprisoned in the past. It was time to make my love greater than my pain.

Working through this self-forgiveness process, I began to feel lighter. Even though no words had been exchanged between us, my attitude had gone through a major adjustment. I no longer felt angry at him or at myself. I felt peaceful and ready to meet him with a clear heart.

It is never too late to drop off the end of the screw and be free. That said, no one can make that final turn for us. Only we can forgive ourselves and let go.

Daily Practices

Forgiveness Inquiry

What stops you from forgiving? How do you think not forgiving serves you? What do you imagine will happen if you
forgive, that serves as such a strong inhibitor to such a pro-
foundly freeing act? What is the cost of not forgiving? Consider becoming willing to forgive even if you do not know
how right now. Think of a possible way to bring forgiveness
into a relationship in your family or workplace. Imagine what
freedom will come if you move into the blessing of forgiveness. Try taking one breath of forgiveness now.

Clearing Karma Meditation

Sit comfortably and begin deep rhythmic breathing. When
you feel relaxed, bring to mind someone with whom you feel
unresolved karma or conflict. Imagine that person sitting in
front of you at a safe distance. Then bring your awareness
back to your own body and breath. Slowly move your attention from the top of your head, down your face and throat,
down your chest and abdomen, to the root of the pelvis, sensing where the energetic cords run between you.

Once you notice a place that holds energy, sense in which
direction the cord initiates—is it from you running over and
hooking into the other person? Or is it from the person running over and hooking into you? Wherever the hook is, gently disengage the energetic cord and draw it back into you if
it is your energy, or send it back to the other person if it is

his. As you do this, see and feel all unhealthy, negative energy being released. Ask that all karma between you be fully and finally completed. Rest assured that if there is love between you, it will not be erased by this exercise.

This is an intentional undoing of the cords of karma that bind us to one another in limiting ways. For each place that energy has either been withdrawn or released, place your hands over that body part and affirm your complete wholeness in love. This exercise will help free you and the other person, and can be done as many times as needed until you no longer feel cords of energy running between you.

Forgiveness meditation

Make yourself comfortable and close your eyes. Relax your face. Relax your mind. Breathe. Imagine someone whom you have had conflict or disagreement with, someone who has obstructed your life in some way, someone you have been withholding love from. Briefly acknowledge your feelings, projections, and thoughts about them. Imagine what your life would be like if you let go of anger and resentment and instead extended love toward them. Really feel what it might be like to be free of this anger, resentment, or hurt. Consider forgiving them.

Now visualize this person who has wronged you in their true nature as love. See the infinite love within the other person's soul. Imagine them surrounded and filled with divine light. Breathe in compassion for their human lack of love awareness. Open your heart and release all expectations and judgments. Bless them with thoughts of peace and harmony. Bless yourself with the same. Are you willing to release this person and free yourself? Release yourself by blessing and releasing them. Release yourself by forgiving them.

PART TWO

············

Filling Up

············

You live that you may learn to love.
You love that you may learn to live.
No other lesson is required of Man.

Mikhail Naimy

Summary

To be free, we must clear the restrictions in our hearts, release fear and anger, be vulnerable to love, and trust it. When we have created this open heart space, we become aware that there is actually a deep well of love filling us from *within.* Times of grief and loss, transition and change, give us the opportunity to know that we are ever sustained by love. From this new perspective, we begin imagining a fresh reality based on ever-active loving and leave a legacy of abundance behind when we depart.

Chapter Ten

....

Developing Eyes of Love

So, it really manifests this way: at first sight,
we find love; at our first true seeing,
the love that is already there touches us.
Mark Nepo

The more devoted we become to practicing love, the more vigilant we must be in monitoring the ways in which the small self tries to limit us. The ego loves to filter all our experiences and interactions based on its selfish needs and desires. Because we all want personal love that will fill us where we still feel empty inside, we assess how people look at us and whether they are sending signals of connection or disregard. We subconsciously seek love from friends, lovers, teachers, and strangers, reconfiguring and redefining it as we go along.

To find what we are longing for, it is time to develop a totally new way of engaging with the world. We must commit to seeing every person through eyes of love, whether we know them or not, whether we like them or not, whether they are being kind to us or not, every day with no exception. This requires a dedication to love, *no matter what.*

Although it may seem difficult to fathom, take a deep breath and relax. It does not have to happen overnight.

A New Worldview

The key lies in separating the emotional waves of personal love from the consistent energy of pure love. On a human level, when we "have eyes for someone" we fall "in love." We respond to something they are reflecting to us, something we need: validation, support, empathy, fun, or companionship. When they give us some pleasure, we experience the feeling of love for them, but what we are really doing is nurturing our own ego, which has been pleased by them. As soon as they are not available physically or emotionally to feed our need, we feel less loved or less lovable. If they stop giving us pleasure altogether, our love for them usually wanes. Basically, if we are thinking "I need you," it is based on selfishness, not pure love. This is why sexual attraction does not equal love. The sexual impulse drives desire and clouds our ability to see clearly. Desire propels us into relationships and often when we are no longer being satisfied in the same way, it pulls us out again.

The ego mind will forever believe that fulfillment lies "out there" and relentlessly pursue hit after hit of pleasure. But the soul knows that pure love does not come through satiating the senses. If it did, promiscuity would have gotten us all to enlightenment by now.

The effortless emotional high of sexual attraction is simply the dance of the ego trying to experience love by posturing for what it can get rather than what it can give; and its effect is as impermanent as any drug. Inevitably, the trick of brain biochemistry that creates the euphoric feelings of new love goes away within two years, on average. We are left feeling unloved because we have mistakenly believed that the other person is the ultimate source of love.

Long-term happiness requires shifting from satisfaction seeking to sharing true intimacy and spiritual development. When sounded aloud, the word "intimacy" can be heard as "into-me-see," a lovely reminder about what we are doing when we get close to someone. We are attempting to see beyond his ego's mask and inviting him to do the same, into our shared nature as love. Intimacy is not just physical togetherness. It is the deep at-one-ness that blooms in our consciousness when we experience our own or another person's essence. We can walk by the same person a hundred times and not really see him, or we can walk by once, and completely take him in, *if* our eyes are focusing through the lens of love.

As we learn to see others through eyes of love, we spiritualize human relationship, and sexual connection. The sweetness of this is far stronger than any fleeting passion. Passion can be enhanced *by* love, but it should not be mistaken *for* love. Without spiritual love in an intimate, physical relationship, consciousness remains at its lowest level and eventually attraction, respect, and understanding can erode. Even long-term marriages become stale and lose their perceived value when too much focus is on the physical rather than on seeing one another as reflections of pure love.

Making the shift to see through eyes of love takes a courageous act of willpower to elevate our thoughts and regulate the senses, which continuously shout enticements to indulge them at any cost. A breathing exercise that can help us do this is included at the end of the chapter.

Purifying the Heart

To change our focus from the physical to the spiritual dimension requires a process of purifying our hearts. There are stages to this, and the practices of meditation that have already been shared help clear us so we can overcome impulses and habits that take us away from divine love.

When we begin life, the first stage is naturally self-centered: physical needs and desires, emotional attachment, and the demand of fulfillment from caregivers. Unfortunately, some people stay in this stage forever. But as we begin to awaken, we see that to remain exclusively self-serving does not bring ultimate fulfillment. Then we start to seek real knowledge.

In I Corinthians in the Bible are some beautiful guidelines on how to practice a wiser love, described as patient and kind, never envious, proud, or boastful. Selfless love does not dishonor others, is not easily angered, and keeps no record of wrongs. It does not delight in evil but rejoices with the truth. It always protects, always trusts, always hopes, and always perseveres (I Corinthians 13:4–8).

To embody these actions and attitudes of love, especially when someone is unkind, or even hurtful to us, we need to have clear and determined eyes of love. Again, this does not mean we condone or accept evil actions. It means that we bear witness to the souls within those confused humans who have become so forgetful of their true nature and so detached from truth that they have forsaken love. Rather than react or retaliate, we pause. We breathe. Then we shift our focus and look with our eyes of love, beyond the exterior ego they are showing us, to the soul that is hidden beneath the outer display of ignorance.

At this stage, we discover how good it feels to overcome the self-centered ego and help others. We no longer allow the senses to strip us of our inner power. An unselfish, mutual love blooms in the heart, and our relationships deepen and become a catalyst for spiritual evolution. Consideration for each other becomes more important than any emotional or physical attraction.

The Spiritual Practice of Loving

Although it is not easy to keep the heart softly open or the eyes gently focused on love, it is *possible*, and we begin where we can begin. If we do not, then we risk closing our hearts in either despair or outrage. By starting somewhere, we prevent fear and rage from robbing us of our inner peace. Any small gesture of love changes us for the better and changes the world in the same breath.

Every time we look through eyes of love, we see that there is only one energy of love shining through different faces and physiques. Source love is playing hide-and-seek with us in a million different disguises, through every human expression of love we share with partners, relatives, and friends. It is visible in each spark of affection or attention and hiding again with every rejection or denial.

Each relationship we are blessed with gives us an opportunity to practice loving in different and ever-expanding ways, the challenge being to return to the essence of love itself and stop concentrating on whether the spark is on or off. This is the *sadhana*, the spiritual practice of loving. It is not an intellectual exercise but a meditation on our shared oneness twenty-four hours a day, every day.

When the ecstatic and effortless state of falling in love has ended, we dive deeper into the intimacy of seeing one another as love. We focus on what we can offer to others in service to their souls. We think, "How can I contribute to this other person's happiness and spiritual growth? How can I love beyond what feeds my needs and desires?" We give love as a gift from our hearts without expecting anything in return, desiring only our beloved's true happiness. This creates a calm, inward satisfaction, purposefully connected to something greater than self.

In the final stage of purifying the heart, we extend the practice of loving beyond our closest circles and consciously try to love everyone. We begin seeing every challenging family member, nasty neighbor, or back-stabbing coworker through a new love filter and work toward extending compassion to the souls of even the violent, hate-filled people in the world.

Do Not Stop Now

This may seem terribly difficult, especially given the fear and conflict present in the world today. I can feel the skepticism and even dread arising as you read these words. I can feel them because I have known them in my own heart. I faced them when I chose to write this book, and I face them *every* time I am challenged by the painful limitations of my human love. This is the ultimate challenge to the awakened individual. It is the call to spiritualize every moment of our lives by living the principle of love.

The active practice of seeing through eyes of love is a leap into the faith that love holds the answer to *everything*. That said, it is a big leap, and if we do not know how to begin, just being willing to consider it is wonderful.

To make conscious loving our life goal and purpose for doing anything, whether the world responds or turns away enables us to carry on with passion and purpose. Loving becomes our guiding philosophy, sustaining us during times of sorrow and discouragement, giving us meaning and joy. It may be a big mountain to climb, and it may seem simpler to slide back into complacency or reactivity. But there is no turning back once we begin—there is only more love.

Daily Choice

Whether we are in an intimate relationship or not, we can practice loving each person we encounter on a daily basis. By choosing love as the basis for all our thoughts and actions, we not only dramatically benefit the relationships shared with spouses, parents, friends, children, and colleagues, but we also affect countless strangers as well.

When we stop following our fluctuating feelings and personal desires, we grow beyond the emotional chemical reaction firing in our brains that we thought of as love in the past. We recognize love as the peace within our own being and see that what we seek is *who we are*. Aligned with this all-encompassing, ever-available, and limitless love, we cannot help but love what is around us, and this effects immediate transformation.

The reason Jesus taught to love with all our minds, hearts, and souls is because we activate a powerful and constructive force when we do so. Love is the greatest influencer for positive change. Every moment becomes different when we open the inner vision based in pure spiritual love. Where before we saw limitation, now we see possibility. Where before we felt anger or fear, now we only feel compassion. And where we felt discouraged, now we imagine infinite potential.

By removing the filters in our own consciousness that keep us from universal, undifferentiated love, we feel more joy in our relationships now and as they change in the future.

Eventually, as we expand beyond the personal limitations of love, offering our understanding and empathy not just to those closest to us but to all mankind, the whole world becomes our beloved. We know love as a daily choice, an orientation to life that infuses how we listen, speak, and act. Then the purified heart is free from all belief in being separate, and we have an unobstructed inner experience of divine love. Falling into love with the love within and around us in every moment, we feel deeply and truly joyful.

A Personal Story

When my son was little, we lived alone one winter on an unpopulated beach in New England. Our house had big glass windows looking out over the sand dunes. Beautiful and expansive during the day, the house felt eerily dark and quiet at night since there were no other residents around. One evening I had tucked my son in as usual and proceeded to work for several more hours on the computer. As it neared midnight and I prepared to finally head to bed, one last email popped in from an unknown address. Thinking it was a work inquiry, I opened it and was instantly horrified—the email consisted of a photo of me and a message threatening my life.

Staring at the computer, surrounded by the darkness of the deserted beach outside, I felt a wave of terror run through me. I had no enemies and could not fathom how such a message of hatred would land on my desk. The sender was unidentified and the email address was unfamiliar to me, yet the words were personalized in a way that led me to believe I knew the individual somehow. I lay awake in fear that night, pondering who it could be, why this was happening, and how I could protect my son and myself.

With a clearer mind the next day, it came to me who was likely behind the threat. I took the email to the police and filed a report naming the person I suspected, but doing so did not make the fear go away. In fact, it was all I could think about. Terrorism comes in many forms, from abuse in families to random acts of violence in society including political wars that rage around us. Each of us has things in our lives that threaten to make us crumble in fear and hate. I knew that if I let it, this random act of terrorism could stop me from living a joyful, free life. I did not want to feel this constraint or distrust those around me. I did not want to hate this individual.

I decided not to give fear power over my mind. Every time the message or the person who had sent it came into my thought, I sent them a silent blessing of peace. I saw myself surrounded by a protective bubble of light and this person in another one. I knew that it was because of their own inner confusion that they could possibly have sent such a horrible message to me. I only allowed myself to think of good things I knew about the person I suspected and sent love in the universal way, from soul to soul. I prayed that they would be free of the darkness that clouded their knowing of love, refusing to see the person through eyes of fear or hate. I had to be diligent daily in my thought whenever they came to mind. Even now I know I could indulge fear, but I choose to send peace and see only through eyes of love.

Daily Practices

Heart Sight

Close your eyes and forget about your physical sight. Feel into your inner sight, your heart sight. Think of someone in your life that you have conflict with. Put yourself in a protective bubble of pure love and put the other person in one as well. Practice looking beyond their ego mask to the love that is their essential being. Notice how this feels. Try this in your daily outer life as well, especially with anyone who presents a challenge.

Connect Sexual Feelings to the Heart

Try this powerful exercise next time you feel a sexual impulse in the physical body that is unconnected to pure love. Begin slow full breathing. Draw the physical sensation of arousal from the genitals up to the heart center. Put your entire focus on the heart, and breathe love in and out from there until you feel the sensations in the lower body connect with the love in your heart. If you are with a partner, take twelve slow, deep breaths and look into her eyes, seeing her soul.

Beholding Meditation

This can be done with another person or with yourself in a mirror. Find a quiet space and time where you will not be interrupted for at least five minutes. Gaze into the light in the pupils of your partner's or your own eyes. Release all thought, and just be in full attentive presence. Concentrate on the energy, the love that is within you both, the same love at the level of pure awareness.

Eyes of Love Exercise

Set an intention to be fully present with others today and to look at everyone through the eyes of love. Take people in; their eyes, their energy. Appreciate the connection between you, how the same energy beats in their heart as it does in your own. Hold your heart open regardless of what they offer to you. If you are experiencing conflict or alienation from someone you love, visualize both of your hearts being opened and touched by the transforming power of divine love in a way that limited human love cannot. See a benevolent outcome dissipating the conflict between you. Consciously hold them and yourself in the inner vision of love.

Chapter Eleven

....

Deepening Meditation through Devotion

*Unselfish love for all people without
exception is the most important point
of convergence among all significant
spiritualities and religions.*
Stephen G. Post, PhD

It takes great endurance to keep coming back to the practice of conscious loving day after day. We all get tired and discouraged and fall back into patterns driven by our egos. Yet each time we see ourselves as separate from one another or prioritize the protection of the small self, we move away from love. Day by day, we build the strength and the commitment to take loving to the next level.

To do this, meditation is essential. If you have not already established a regular routine for sitting meditation, now is the time. Our dedicated meditation practice reinforces our ability to remain devoted to the sadhana of loving. Will you prioritize time for meditation or always crowd it out with other things? Will you give in to distraction on the cushion or remain focused and faithful? Will you hold the person in your life who is presenting you with a challenge as an impediment or as a doorway to greater loving?

On the Cushion

Through consistent meditation, we establish a relationship with love that then sustains us during difficult times in life. But just like when you are dating, there is a process of getting to know one another before we feel ready to dedicate our time and our hearts. Until we totally know love, it is difficult to be completely devoted to it.

Where our heart is, our mind follows. Whatever we care about the most, we are naturally devoted to and serve. Our actions reflect our intentions. We show devotion through the time and attention we spend on things or people. What do you prioritize; your work, your church, your social media, your dog? Look objectively at how you manage time and energy and you will see what you value most.

Prioritizing Love

The more we meditate, the more we feel love's presence within our own hearts and the more devoted we become. We prioritize it in every conversation, every interaction, every project.

We keep our thought on love throughout the day and look for more and more ways to express it to those around us, even—or especially—when they are not doing the same!

If our partner or child is in a rotten mood and acting rudely, we meet them with loving understanding and compassionate boundaries rather than reactivity. We offer generosity to strangers through a kind word or gesture for no particular reason.

Practicing love becomes a moment by moment choice to love what and who is in front of us to the best of our ability, expecting nothing in return, rather than a monumental act of service or charity.

A circular flow begins between choosing love in our daily activities and becoming absorbed in love in our meditations. One feeds the other, and vice versa. As we practice the presence of love outwardly and prioritize time with it inwardly, then all our thoughts and actions will become devotional.

The more attention we give to love, the more we will manifest it in our relationships, and the more we will know it as our true success and security. We will share more understanding with partners and friends, more genuine listening with our children and colleagues, more compliments with strangers, and more authentic feelings with our families.

How to Get There

Discipline is required to initiate both loving and meditating, but devotion keeps us coming back. Devotion holds no self-interest and no expectations. There is no fear in devotion, only trust. The more we offer up the inner defenses and surrender our personal love to the universal Source of love, the more we create a relationship with that which we are seeking. Thankfully, no matter how weary or discouraged we may feel, we will be met with the reassuring presence of love if we come to our meditation time with an open heart.

If we affirm "I am here for you, love. What can I offer you today?" rather than think "What can I get out of this? What have you got for me today?" we will awaken greater devotion in our hearts. As a result, love's response will be even stronger, and we will feel profound peace.

Like any other worthwhile pursuit, deep devotion is a state of being that is cultivated with time and consistent effort. The ego is tenacious in trying to stay in control, which is why we need endurance. Devotion and loyalty grow in our hearts when we concentrate with gratitude on the many forms of love we experience. In our meditation time, we can begin by focusing on anything or anyone that arouses devotion in our hearts.

Think of what you hold dearest: the feeling of being with an intimate partner, trusted friend, innocent child, a pet, or something in nature—something that inspires you now. Build deeper concentration by focusing your whole mind and heart on that aspect of love during your meditation, then let the form fall away in your mind and just hold the energy of divine love in your heart.

We bring devotion back to Source by recognizing every expression of love; every father, mother, child, friend, and lover as an extension of the one universal love. Over time, focused devotion facilitates deeper meditation because it quells the fluctuations of emotions and desires. It creates a quiet peaceful reservoir within us where we can rest and renew ourselves daily. We do not have to manufacture love when we feel depleted—we need only quiet the mind long enough to tap the inner well of it awaiting within.

The more we meditate, the less we will identify with and try to protect the individual self, and thus the more our souls will be able to shine through. Then we experience a passion far more intense than being *in love* humanly. We enjoy the ecstasy of being *inside love*. We realize that we are continuously guided, guarded, provided for, and protected. Realizing this we feel a peace and strength within us, capable of overcoming any life challenge. Every moment becomes a meditation, and love becomes a way of daily living.

Devotion and Loyalty in Relationship

In addition to our dedicated daily sitting practice, we offer devotion to love by making all our human relationships a type of meditation in action. Whoever we converse with during the day becomes a mirror we look into, to see how close or far away we are from pure love. Every interaction serves our spiritual growth, as we move toward unity consciousness by continuously electing kindness, respect, compassion, and thoughtfulness.

Whether physically intimate or not, if two people are dedicated to being psychological, emotional, and spiritual support for each other, then they are practicing devotion to love. Every day brings new ways in which we can see the spiritual essence of our friend or partner even if they are not aware of it themselves. Through unconditional loyalty and dedication to the other person's highest good, it is possible to experience divine love through the microcosm of human love.

In partnerships, we strive to expect less of another and more of ourselves. In intimate physical relationships, we express selfless soul love instead of looking only for sensory gratification or personal validation. We appreciate and acknowledge the goodness in one another, and offer forgiveness when we have conflict. This relationship is based on giving rather than receiving.

Selfishness is one of the biggest hurdles for our egos to overcome on the way to remembering our soul nature. We counteract this by totally and completely devoting ourselves to love through innumerable creative ways outwardly, as well as inwardly in the communion of meditation.

The Devotion to Self

No one said that we need to be perfect at these practices. We all slide into small needy places at times and direct that neediness at one another instead of to love itself. If negative self-talk or exhaustion from our efforts threatens to derail our journey towards love, devotion is the quality that will return our minds to peace and help us refocus on what is most important. Through our development of devotion, we recognize that solutions never lie in the illusory dream of duality but always in *awakening to more love.*

Every day, through the spiritual practice of breathing love, we acknowledge the sacred within ourselves and all those around us. Because we cannot be separated from love, we are never alone, ever. You are not alone, I am not alone, and we are not separate. All experience of separation ends when our only desire is simply to *be* the love that we already are. Both in relationships and in meditation, this is the natural movement of the heart toward Source.

As soon as we surrender the personal "I," love appears as our very own divine Self. It fills us and sustains us and enables us to walk through life with a consciously loving and ever open heart, elevating us to a state of joy unparalleled by material acquisitions, accomplishments, or relationships.

A Personal Story

Tired from traveling for work one summer and in need of some inner nourishment, I showed up significantly early to a live kirtan chanting event in San Diego, excited to see Krishna Das perform. I knew many of his devotional songs by heart and often used them in my yoga classes and personal practice to center me before meditation. I found a seat on the floor, making my little personal nest with a meditation cushion and blanket. I should have closed my eyes and gone inward to a place of stillness and inner connection, but as these are festive events, my attention was drawn outward to the many people greeting one another and the fanciful outfits, tattoos, and jewelry people were wearing.

Since I was away from home, I had no one to talk with so I just listened and watched as the hall got more and more crowded. Abuzz with energy, the throngs of people trying to push their way closer to the stage soon overtook my little meditation nest. I could feel a sense of agitation arising as loud talkers practically sat on top of me, caring little, it seemed, for what was to be an event of devotion and spiritual practice. Edged now to the side of the room and disturbed by the incessant meaningless chatter, I was resentfully hanging on, wishing the program would begin so they would all have to be quiet and I could get a little peace. I needed to be refilled from what had been an exhausting month of teaching and traveling. I wanted to drink in Krishna Das's loving energy of devotion.

The louder the hall got, the more judgmental my mind became about people and their pretentiousness until halfway through the first song, when I had an A-ha! moment. I realized *I* was the one sitting in the wrong place in relation to devotion. I wanted something *from* the practice rather than bringing my love and devotion *to* it. I realized that renewal does not come from drawing something in from the outside but rather from reaching deeper within my own heart to express more devotion and love, thereby overcoming the feeling of depletion, limitation, and alienation from those around me.

In a millisecond, everything shifted. I felt a huge up-surging of love in my heart, and I sang out with more energy and zeal than I realized I had in me. By giving my heart over in devotion, I received the renewal of love. All judgment and concern for those around me disappeared and our voices blended into one harmonious devotional chant to love. By the end of the evening I floated out with the rest of the crowd, feeling totally filled and renewed. This is what we must practice in every challenging, depleting moment of our daily lives, the willingness to love more and trust that we will be filled by offering devotion to those around us.

Daily Practices

Lose Your Self in Love

The surrender of the small self to love is the greatest devotional offering we can make. Today, practice giving up "my" will, needs, desires, beliefs, and thoughts. See what shows up. Try to go one hour without saying or even thinking "I," "me," "my," or "mine." Find ways to serve whoever is in front of you. Seek increasingly to put the ego in service to the soul and to choose love over anything else.

Practices to Spiritualize Love

- See everyone as your teacher, another part of the one love, wearing a disguise to see how you will treat him.

- Remember that anything you do to another, you do to your Self.

- Give only love, kindness and understanding wherever you go.

- Send out only thoughts of love and goodwill, even to those who have hurt you.

- Express appreciation constantly.

- Never close your heart.

Devotion Meditation

In your daily meditation, start by holding someone or something in your heart to whom you feel completely devoted. Devotion draws us back to love. Then let your love expand beyond the boundaries of this personal expression into the limitlessness of divine love itself. Pour your whole heart, mind, and soul onto the altar of love.

Chapter Twelve

....

Recognizing Your
Self as Love

*... enlightenment is the moment
we realize that we are made of love.*

Mark Nepo

We have analyzed the emotions, desires, temptations, and insecurities that keep us from knowing our Self as love, and yet the identification with the small self runs deep. In fact, it is the number one obstacle to a life of true fulfillment. Perceiving ourselves as separate from one another reinforces self-consciousness and causes much suffering and insecurity. Unfortunately, the contemporary model of self-love often feeds this egoic paradigm and in doing so fails to bring inner peace, no matter how many achievements we rack up or how many esteem boosting affirmations we say. Until we shift from the limitation of self-consciousness to the freedom of Self-consciousness, we will always come up short.

The basic perception that there is an "other" is the fundamental problem. As long as we see love through this filter, we will fluctuate between two positions: trying to merge with a separate someone in order to get the love we want from him; and pushing him away to preserve a sense of self that might be compromised in the relationship. Both of these decisions are based on the mistaken polarization of self and other.

It is time to find union within our own consciousness, because only then can we merge in compassionate presence with another, recognizing ourselves as one, and Self as all. Ultimately, we must lose our self *in* love to find it again *as* love.

The way to know our true nature is by moving deeper into the energetic experience of living and being love. We need to stop *thinking about* love, and start *sensing it* within our hearts where it has always existed. Just like the wave which is an inseparable part of the ocean, our individualized self is an inextricable part of the eternal Self, which is love. The ocean may exist without waves but the wave cannot exist without the ocean.

What we need at this point is complete dedication to knowing self and other not as separate, struggling beings but as aspects of the one great Self. It is time to see ourselves clearly through eyes of love and remember fully who we are.

Living Inside Love

As we awaken to our inherent connection, rather than directing the love we feel toward people with an agenda of having it reciprocated back to us, we can practice loving all who come on our path as a gesture of loving love itself. This can be done whether we are in human partnership or not. If we love the love that exists within all beings, then we see beyond personalities, forms, and egos, to the indwelling essence. Then we hold universal sympathy for all beings, and love beyond personal agendas and desires. As a result we feel a totally new level of joy.

This undifferentiated loving becomes a circular flow satiating us from within. It is the only way to true fulfillment, because no other human can reciprocate as clearly and completely as pure love can. This is the love of Source for all its creations, the inaudible voice of the soul heard in the stillness of meditation. Any love that shines toward us or that we offer to another is only possible because of Source love. All the million varied expressions have but one origin. All love, power, thought, and breath come from the One. We are but instruments, channels of the great love and its perfection is already within us.

The goal is to become so clear and ego-surrendered that love flows unobstructed through us, dissolving all walls of separation, illuminating our path to enlightenment. When our consciousness finally expands beyond the small self-identity, there are no words to fully describe what awaits. It is a total recalibration of who we think we are.

Beyond the personal self that is defined by thoughts and feelings is a spacious, ever-expanding is-ness. As we let go of the mental constructs that preserve and express the personality, what arises is the natural, harmonious state of our inner being, which is love. It is an uncontainable, indescribable state of being that is harmonious and still. In it, we feel a relaxed, detached sense of trust in whatever is happening, and a strong commitment to be present in each moment to do our special part. Here we find a similarity in all people, places, roles, and goals, yet there is a deep joyfulness in each unique expression.

The Doorway Home

As we remove the barriers created by the ego self, love radiates brilliantly through us and we meet it more all around us. Whether we ever have the "perfect" intimate relationship becomes less important than whether we can move deeper into the realization of who we are as eternal spiritual beings. To reach this expansive state, we must seek silence and leave the thinking mind behind.

Daily meditation puts us in touch with the endless spring of love within and we no longer have to be satisfied with fleeting tastes of love externally. Each time we stop the outer quest and walk through the inner doorway of meditation, we find greater joy and clearer love. A guided meditation in appendix 1 supports this turning back to true Self.

At a certain point, no more words can be applied to this experience. Love cannot be brought into understanding through thought, only through presence. With time and focused, selfless efforts in meditation, we cease having to think about ourselves as *being* love, we simply exist in the knowing that *it is so*. Eventually, we become so absorbed in love that there is no more you or me, only love. Then we can say "I love, because I *am* love."

A Personal Story

I knew a photographer once who could look through his camera lens into the eyes of his subject and draw forth their most beautiful inner essence. He knew how to put people at ease and connect soul to soul. He was passionate and enthusiastic, having the energy of a little child. He took time to listen to who people really were and he looked through eyes of love when he snapped the shutter. As a result, he was able to capture the beauty within each subject for the rest of the world to see. His portraits were distinctly different from any other I have ever seen.

He took my picture once and our conversation flowed on beyond the photo session. We had common thoughts on books, relationships, and spirituality, so we went for tea. He was nineteen years older than me and had a lot more life under his belt than I did at the time. I was intrigued by both the edge and the softness in him that I had never before encountered, particularly within the same human being. We became close friends and spent many hours discussing the difficulties of being human, how to understand ourselves, have successful relationships, and how to know God. He had a personal drive toward self-knowing and enlightenment that made him at times tender and at other times relentless with himself. But he was wise and loving, and I was drawn into his understanding, compassionate heart.

He helped me see the ways in which I was not honoring myself in the relationship I was in at that time. He also pointed out how my soul was suffering because I had disowned my own experience of God and connection to love. He awakened in me a realization that there was far more to love than I knew, and the desire to know it completely. He did this not by wooing me with his personal love but by loving me in a selfless way that only wanted my happiness and spiritual awakening. As a result, I felt a different type of joy in his presence, not the giddy in-love feeling of new relationships, but a calm presence of joy unconnected from need-based human love. I experienced more love simply holding his hand than I had in any previous intimate relationship.

One day we met early for coffee and as we parted he gave me a long hug and then put a box in the back seat of my car. He told me to open it later. We were always exchanging books and other inspirational things so I looked forward to seeing what was inside when I had time that evening. Later on, as I finished up the day's appointments, I checked my messages and heard his voice sharing something about a book we had been discussing that morning. He said, "I think if you look in some of the places in your own heart where there are holes, hurts, and wounds and you heal them, then you will find that your experience of love will change."

He concluded with words I will never forget. "I am going to go away, and I will not be back. I just want you to remember that I love you; my choices are mine, and you are not responsible. Just see me as a big lesson. I hope that one of the things that you got out of this relationship was to know what it feels like to be in love with love with another human being. I hope if you got something from me, that is what you got. I love you, Jennie. I will be with you in spirit always."

I do not know what was more intense in that moment, the piercing pain in my chest or the screaming in my mind. Going away? He owned a business and a home—he couldn't just drop everything and leave for a trip. Was he telling me he no longer wanted contact with me? With adrenaline pumping and thoughts swirling, I drove to his house immediately.

The door was locked. Feeling a growing sickness in my gut, I reached out to the only person I knew might have been in contact with him, his ex-wife. When she picked up the phone, I could tell she was shaken too. He had left her a handwritten note that day as well, saying goodbye.

The next few hours were surreal. I went to her house, we called the police, and then we waited as they searched for him. At dusk, the call came saying that he had been found in a state park where we used to picnic and hike. We drove there not knowing what we were going to find, and were met by police officers and a canine unit. He had been found dead, a bullet to his heart by his own hand.

The details between that moment of discovery and when we left the park are unclear in my memory now, but twenty-four years later, I can still feel the sadness. I recall sitting in my car sobbing, wanting only to follow him wherever he had gone, unable to bear the thought of life without the man who opened my heart to true love. I could not fathom how someone who embodied so much wisdom and love could have put a bullet through his own heart ... and broken mine into a million pieces.

It has taken me more than two decades to write this down and although I have thought at length about it, I will never fully understand his choice. What I do realize now is that although he seemed to understand love intellectually, he did not know *himself as love*. Knowing ourselves in this manner is the critical difference for all of us; it is what makes it possible to bear the pain of being human. It is the only thing that makes life meaningful.

In his message to me, he had it backward: we do not heal the wounds in our hearts to change our experience of love. When we decide to make our love greater than our pain, a pure unconditional love comes into us and heals our wounded hearts. The mind cannot grasp how this can happen, but the soul knows that it does.

Daily Practices

Who Am I Meditation

Find a quiet place to lie down and relax. Adjust the body so everything is completely at ease. Pay attention to your breath and adjust the rhythm of the breath so it becomes slow and deep. Place your awareness in the center of the chest around the heart. Feel the inner beating of the heart and sense the life force energy moving through your veins. Ask yourself, "Who am I?"

Feel the breath moving through the entire body, slowly and deeply. Ask yourself again, "Who am I?" Sense into the space around the edges of the body, feeling how your physical self connects to the space around you, and inquire again within, "Who am I?" Let your perception dwell on the brain, all the synapses and neurons firing. Ask again, "Who am I?" Think of the spaces that you have moved through all during your life. Ask "Who am I?" Sense all the feelings that have ever come through your being. Ask, "Who am I?" Then let all these associations go and ask, "Who am I really?"

Opening the Heart Meditation

Sit comfortably with an erect spine and relax the entire body. Start to breathe slowly and deeply. Place your inner gaze at the third eye point and imagine the breath is entering there. Simultaneously become aware of the heart center and imagine that the breath is exiting from there. Breathing into the third eye, breathing out of the heart. How does this flow feel? Spend five or more minutes here.

Self-reflection Exercise

- What has changed about your understanding of love?

- What do you now believe about your self and love?

- How will you remain focused on this rather than any old story about love?

Chapter Thirteen

....

Grief and Loss: Letting Go and Loving On

Love is the only medicine that will
heal the wounds of the world.
Mata Amritanandamayi (Amma)

Throughout life, we grieve any loss of human love through separation, change, or death. Even when we choose a parting that we know is for the best, we still grieve, and each loss we experience can compound painfully in our hearts. Because grief is uncomfortable, many people want to avoid it, and many doctors prescribe anti-depressants to those in the normal grieving process to lessen the symptoms of loss.

It may not seem like it, but grief is a powerful portal to awareness, an opportunity to know ourselves anew when an old version of self is phasing out. It is our system's natural, emotional, healing process. It has inherent value because when experienced fully, normal grief breaks our hearts open wider, enabling us to love more than we were capable of previously.

Though everyone feels grief on a more regular basis than they might admit, we are rarely taught *how* to grieve, unfortunately. By understanding the similarities in all forms of grief, we can better contextualize our feelings and understand how to be with them when loss arrives. Each person's grieving process is unique, but the experience is universally human.

Cleaning the Wound

When we lose someone we love, nothing is as it was before, and no one likes change when it is forced upon them. A wounded heart is as raw and vulnerable as a wounded body. And just as the body takes time to repair itself, the heart also takes time to heal.

The first response to any loss is often shock coupled with numbness or lack of feeling. As a little time passes, the common physical sensations of grief begin: heaviness in the heart center, a disorganized mind, and a general lack of energy. It is normal to be irritable, irrational, unfocused, depressed, tired, anxious, withdrawn, lonely, sad, scared, and emotionally volatile.

The grieving process is a series of ups and downs with no definitive timeline and no rationale. We might feel angry at being suddenly alone and forced into a change of life structure, or outraged at the injustice of a disease, accident, or betrayal. We may also fear our own impending mortality or further loss of others close to us.

We need to be gentle with ourselves when grieving, accepting all our feelings. This is how we clean the wounded heart. Just as we would flush out a physical wound so it does not get infected, we need to get out all the emotional reactions to our loss by talking about our loved ones, writing them letters, or creating tributes of love to them. Plenty of rest is needed as well as fresh air, exercise, healthy food, and moral support.

Daily meditation is especially healing, as it offers time and space to witness all that arises. We can be with the intensity of each moment of grief, offering gentle presence to ourselves as the heart heals. Through stillness, we can return to the pure love within where we are always connected.

Transmuting Grief to Love

At the same time we are feeling our natural human feelings, we can recognize that they only exist because we are grieving for *ourselves*, *our* loss, what *we* miss, *our* attachment, rather than for the one who has died or gone away. It is attachment rather than love that fuels our grief. We grieve the loss of continuity of relationship with our loved ones. But love itself can never be lost.

If a beloved person in our life has died, we can recognize that although the body has left, the love between us lives on. Rather than crumble under a crushing sense of grief, we can focus on encouraging the person to go onto their next adventure with our strength and support, knowing that one day we will meet again. Instead of focusing on the loss, it is far better to send the departed our love and desire for their continued happiness and offer our love to others who are still near. If we do not do this, they may feel our sorrow and heaviness, and we risk closing our hearts to protect against the possibility of further loss.

As we offer our personal attachments and grief, our limited human love can transform into pure love. We do not make grief go away by stifling our life or our love, nor can we bring someone back who has died or left us in another way. But if we are resilient and create meaning within loss by electing to love again, we honor our relationship with the one who has gone. If we fill the empty spaces in our hearts with pure love, we can liberate ourselves from sadness and feel, through the silent language of the heart, the continuity maintained between souls who have been dear to us.

Letting Go and Loving On

There is a spiritual law that to receive love, we must give love to those who need it. Times of loss when we feel particularly needy are wonderful opportunities to practice greater giving of love through understanding, kindness, and compassion. We are the ones who benefit most when we ask caring questions of those around us, such as "What do you need?" or "How can I help you?" When we feel upset or limited in our capacity to love others, we must compassionately remember that we *are* love itself.

Moments of happiness and sorrow pass. People come in and out of our lives. Our paths change course. We cry and then rejoice. As we practice mindful loving in daily life, we no longer pray for obstacles to be removed so much as for the strength to overcome them, and for love to increase in our hearts. We realize that the only reason we fear anything is because we have not leaned completely into the strength and solace of love.

Love is Joy

The only way to fully quench our deep longing for love is to think and speak and act from deeper and purer love every day, regardless of how much we feel we have lost personally. Seeing through eyes of love, we honor all souls as part of the vast ocean of love that is far greater than any bodily form.

This is the reunification of our consciousness with the awareness that we are all unconditional love in our core essence. Connected to the center of our being through devotion and meditation, we feel more ease and joy, and experience the eternal love we desire. Losses will still happen in the physical realm where nothing lasts forever, but we are sustained knowing that we are love.

A Personal Story

Ending relationships is never easy, but it is particularly difficult when we love the person dearly. I had been in a long-term relationship with a man I loved very much, yet the time came when I knew deep in my soul that I could no longer share human partnership with him. Although we connected in so many ways, especially through our spiritual intentions and beliefs, I felt we were not compatible in daily life. I had agonized over the decision to end the relationship for years, always hoping for some outward shift to occur that would make things smoother. We had shared beautiful times together...and painful ones too.

He did not agree with my choice to end the relationship and he was bitter and hurt, as we all are when things we want end. The fighting between us escalated until one day I begged him to just go, so that we did not destroy every last bit of love left between us. I deeply wanted to continue loving him, even if I did not want to be with him physically.

The parting was painful, and we both grieved the loss of the personal love we had shared for so many years. Our hearts closed to one another at first in an attempt to protect us from more pain, as it would for anyone who has lost a beloved relationship or even a deeply held dream. In our newly separated lives, we each dedicated ourselves to self-development work and our spiritual practice of meditation. Slowly, openings of the heart occurred. We did not communicate much, but I began sending him thoughts of peace and pure love and felt he was sending the same to me.

Many years have passed since that ending, and I believe we have both learned that by keeping the heart open in the very moments it feels hardest to do so—the midst of sorrow, suffering, and loss—we can overcome personal attachments and quell grief by expanding further into divine love. Although we are not close now, he has opened his heart again in non-personal and unconditioned love to me and I to him. We have transformed the love between us from a personal one of shared life experiences to one of pure goodwill and desire for the other's spiritual evolution.

It was not easy to get to where we are, and we both have had times of wishing things turned out differently. But our hearts are now wide open in love, and we share that with all who come into our lives. Our common intention to love beyond the ego's desires has enabled us to offer a purer love to one another and to the world. It is a blessing for everyone.

Daily Practices

Releasing Sorrow

When heavy emotions weigh on your heart, pressing it to close in self-protection, repeat one or all of these affirmations:

- May my love be greater than my pain.
- May my love be greater than my fear.
- May my love be greater than my despair.
- May my love be greater than my anger.
- May my love be greater than my suffering.
- May my love grow stronger with every breath.

Meditation on Aum

The primal vibratory sound *aum* experienced within the mind and body during meditation quiets the restless ego, connects us to divine consciousness, and draws us back to love. Make yourself comfortable and sit with an upright spine. Gently close your eyes and relax. Take a few slow, deep breaths and audibly sound the mantra aum (pronounced "ah—oh—mm") several times, using the fullness of each breath so that you feel its vibration through your body and mind. Then allow the repetition of the mantra to become silent. With each inhalation, silently repeat aum in your mind, elongating the syllable as you did when it was audible, slowly using the whole in-breath. Then with the exhalation, do the same, silently sounding the aum. Repeat for several minutes. Then simply listen for its echo within. Eventually the vibration spontaneously arises and we hear love's voice like a rushing wave soothing our souls.

Connecting Through Love

The point at the center of the forehead just above and between the eyebrows is called the third eye, and it is considered the center of intuition and higher awareness. If we gently turn our internal gaze up to the point with eyelids closed, we can experience a different level of wisdom, one not reliant upon the rational mind. Through this intuitive portal we can also connect telepathically with those we love. If you are missing someone who has left your life, you can connect to that person through love by focusing on the third eye point intently and broadcasting your heartfelt love to them. They will receive the telepathic message of your love, and you should feel greater peace and ease from any grief that may have been present.

Chapter Fourteen

....

Creating a Legacy of Love

We shall forever return to the arms
of those we love, whether our parting is
overnight or over death. The only
thing that lasts is love.
Richard Bach

The ancient Egyptians considered the heart to be the center of thought, memory, and emotion. When a person died, it was believed their heart would be weighed on a scale balanced by a feather that represented the ideals of justice and rightness in conduct. If the heart was heavier than the feather, that meant it was weighted with wrongdoings, so that soul would not enter the afterlife. While not true from a physical standpoint, this is a beautiful metaphor for determining what we need to hold in our hearts and what we need to release. If we want our spiritual hearts to be as light as feathers when we die, anything other than love should be let go.

Why Wait Until You Are Dying

Death never seems to be a welcome subject, yet at a certain point in every human life, there is nowhere left to go and nothing left to do. We will all die. And change happens fast. One day we are here, and the next day we or someone we love is gone.

At this time, our nation is aging rapidly and death rates are increasing. The population over age sixty-five is estimated to double between 2012 and 2050 according to the US Census Bureau. More people are receiving hospice care than ever before and choosing to die at home. Many of us will experience this ourselves, or with a parent or loved one. We are all affected by death because it is an integral part of life. For this reason, we should embrace it as completely and as consciously as we embrace birth. Both life and death are spiritual journeys, journeys of love to be celebrated.

Until we accept the reality that we are all in the process of dying daily, we cannot live or love fully. Furthermore, we will not die in peace unless we know that we have fully lived and fully loved. By recognizing the inevitability of death as part of life, we can clarify our priorities now, create more fulfilling and loving lives, and establish a peaceful relationship with death when it arrives.

Facing Death With a Clear Heart

Many people gain amazing clarity and make huge strides in their spiritual evolution as they near death. They often become more open to love, more willing to forgive, and more apt to consider whether they are leaving a legacy of love behind. The once-ignored deeper questions of life suddenly take on great importance. Additionally, whatever fears have been present become exacerbated.

The consciousness with which we live is the same with which we shall die. Ask yourself, if you were to be faced with death today, would you face it with a consciousness of fear, or one of love?

If we have the luxury of examining our own mortality before it is actually our time to let go of our physical bodies, we can decide to spend our life *doing* what we hope will be remembered in our eulogies. To begin, it helps to consider the questions people typically ask themselves when they know they are dying. These allow us to see what we should be focusing on now to prepare ourselves for an easeful transition from the body, and a heartfelt passing on of love.

Take a moment to reflect upon the following questions:

- How well have I lived?
- What was my life's greatest purpose?
- Did I fulfill it?
- What do I regret?
- How well have I loved?
- Could I love more in the time I have left?

One of the biggest regrets reported by those who are dying is that they lived by what was expected of them rather than by their own truth. They wish they had expressed their feelings courageously and let themselves be happier. They also wish they had not worked so hard, missing moments of their children's youth or partner's companionship, and they wish they had stayed in touch with friends more.

All these regrets point toward the need to love more now; to love ourselves enough to honor our feelings and needs, and to love others enough to prioritize them and be present. Even small changes such as simplifying our lifestyle to create more time for the people and things that are really important can make profound differences. We can fearlessly speak our truth and lovingly release unhealthy relationships rather than let them drain our lives. We can get our heart's affairs in order by telling those we love what they mean to us, making amends and forgiving one another while there is time.

No one should settle for a mediocre existence or allow unexpressed feelings to fester into dis-ease. It will be far more difficult to die with regret and resentment than it will be to express what we need to in the present moment. We do not have to stay stuck in negative experiences. The choice to be happy and to love is always here, in this very moment.

Being proactive through positive change improves our health and elevates our wellbeing. Now is the time to laugh, to let go and to love totally. Do you think the annoyances and grudges of life will matter when you are on your deathbed? They will not. In the end, it all comes down to love.

Fear of Death Limits Love

The great pain people associate with death is often the result of the ego's psychological attachment to the body, as much or more than it is to physiological pain. Of course, no one wants to feel physical pain, but the actual fear of death that people experience is usually because they believe it is a final annihilation of their self. Our greatest misery, in both life and death, results from the emotional and mental pain of believing in a separate self that can die, rather than knowing our true spiritual Self *as love*.

At death, the soul consciousness is freed again from its temporary embodiment. We need not fear personal annihilation if we recognize that death is nothing more than the switching off of life force from the flesh, a transference of consciousness to another state of awareness. It is a metaphysical experience through which we awaken to a new perception of our spiritual nature. The more we learn to identify with our divine Self now, the less fear we will hold of unknowns such as death or other physical change. And by making peace with the fact that our human bodies will die, we free ourselves from the suffering that fearing death creates.

Being With Dying

Resistance in any form is what creates suffering. It is essential that we take stock of our own attitudes about death, especially if we are involved with someone who is dying, as our fear or lack of acceptance can harm the dying person. We must release all judgment and put any personal beliefs aside to allow the person to have their own unique experience. With the right resolve, even death can be loving, transcendent, and peaceful—a beautiful completion to a life well loved. To be with someone as they face death or to be conscious as we face it ourselves is a gift. It is a chance to fulfill our inner commitments to love.

We can embrace conversations about dying and recognize it as a massive opportunity for healing old wounds and relationships. Yes, these conversations may be difficult to have with those we are attached to, but people have an incredible capacity for transformation during this transition, a capacity to move deeper into an awareness of love.

Talking about death does not mean we are giving up on the other person. On the contrary, we want them to know that they will be loved no matter what. People want to be met and held in their fears of suffering, losing control, becoming a burden, leaving things unfinished, and saying goodbye to loved ones. It takes a lot of energy to avoid something as big as death, and pain is aggravated by fear. Talking helps lessen the fear and pain.

If we are courageous, we can help those who are dying by talking about what has been and what will be, about what is real, and what matters most. Reminiscing reduces feelings of isolation and helps the dying person come to terms with unresolved issues. Open-ended questions are helpful, such as, "Is there anything you want to talk about? What are you thinking about? What do you worry about? Would you like to share a special memory? Can I help you in any way? What do you need to feel at peace?"

Do not be concerned if the things the person shares seem inaccurate or out of order. People tend to repeat where they have unresolved feelings and issues. Just see them through eyes of love and listen compassionately with your heart. Do not push away their fears or concerns, and do not interject your own. By really listening to their responses and their feelings, even if they make you feel uncomfortable, you help them find their own resolution. Let them lead the conversation and end it when they are ready. If tears flow, just be still and allow for silence. Take the sacred moment to open your heart even wider into love and to reflect upon the things you can learn from their sharing.

Just as the dying regret the things they did not do in life, we will certainly regret anything left unsaid with our loved ones. When it is our time to talk, we must be sure to say the important things like "I love you. I forgive you. Please forgive me. Thank you. It is okay to go. We will be okay. We will honor you in this way. You will be missed."

Power of Loving Presence

As physical death draws closer, words become less important, but touch, presence, and the intuitive communication of love are essential. Our caring presence is the greatest gift we can give anyone, to be a compassionate witness to their process. When the end is near, it is not a time for intellect and logic but simply love and communication from the heart. We can meditate near the bedside of a dying loved one, or hold them in our thoughts and communicate intuitively through our meditation if distance separates us. They will surely feel the peace and love and be comforted by it.

Physical pain can be compassionately minimized with medication, but often the emotional fear and its resultant suffering is worse than bodily discomfort. How one experiences death will depend on how well they have participated in life, what unfinished business they have, and how great their fear and resistance is to letting go of the human sense of self.

We can be of great support by helping the person to identify with the consciousness of love that is going to withdraw from the body vessel but still live on. We should continue to remind the dying person that he is more than the body that is passing—he is the love within. This will help alleviate much suffering; even a certain amount of physical pain can be lessened if this awareness is present. A guided meditation on letting go into love is included in appendix 2; it can be read aloud to a loved one who is dying.

Loving Into Death

At a certain point, dying people begin to naturally withdraw themselves from the outer world. This going inward offers the time and space in which they can evaluate their lives. It can look like they are just sleeping as they become less communicative but much healing is happening at the soul level.

People in this state are drawing upon spiritual rather than physical energy for this necessary internal work, and their focus is changing from this world to the next.

Their eyes may appear open but glassy and not really seeing, or they may speak of seeing and hearing things or people on the other side. They are no longer grounded here, but have one foot in each world. Yet even if our loved ones become totally nonresponsive to the outer environment, they can still feel love.

Leaving a Legacy of Love

When we understand the process of natural dying, we can prepare ourselves somewhat for this crucial moment of life. Every daily choice to love contributes to our experience at the end and to the legacy we will leave behind in the world. The more unconditional love we share with one another now, the less we will have to worry about when death is at our door. If we heal the things that separate us from the experience of love now, then we will know ourselves as more than just a disintegrating body.

On a daily basis, we create what will be left behind when we pass on. Are we actively creating a legacy of love? We do this for all those in our lives by choosing love in every moment, looking to give more than we receive, and loving beyond our comfort zones. We do it by disengaging conflict and electing compassion and understanding instead.

Rather than waiting for this chaotic, hurting world to change, we create a love legacy by radically restructuring ourselves and offering up personal attachment so it can be transformed into divine love. As we practice the active loving we have discussed in these chapters, our human needs are met because at the root of every human desire is the soul's need to be reunited with its Self as love. Our journey of loving leads us home.

Passing Into Love

The ultimate expression of who we *are* is seen in our willingness to love. When the physical form closes down and energy begins to withdraw, we will focus the mind completely on love, feel it radiating from our heart center, and penetrating from our third eye. We will remember the immortal nature of our soul as well as the changeless and eternal consciousness and all pain and fear will dissipate. Then we will allow our personal self to fall away peacefully as death opens the door to further life, for there is no end that does not start anew in some other form or way. Love is always creating new ways to express itself and is just waiting to pull us forward if we open our hearts to its grace.

In the stillness of our final meditation, the elements of being human melt back into the sea of consciousness from which they were originally made manifest, and death is experienced as liberation, a return to our true nature as love. Every practice, awareness, and breath of love we have taken in life leads us to this final moment. Free beyond the experience of body, mind, and emotion, the awakened soul passes on gently and merges blissfully into universal love.

A Personal Story

From every loss of a loved one who has departed from my life, I have learned something different yet equally profound. Every loss has been painful, yet they all have eventually drawn me closer to love. The greatest of these losses was my mom. Extraordinary in her faithfulness and complete commitment to my well-being, she had been a steadfast example of true love throughout my life.

I was her only child and we shared a deep bond, although we did not always see eye to eye. She had been blessed with a healthy life and I had never known her to be sick for more than a day or two. So when an MRI revealed metastasized cancer throughout her body at age eighty-three, it was as unexpected as it was sudden. The disease was so rampant that it was untreatable, and we were told she had only a month to live.

That kind of news accelerates everything in life and puts priorities into rapid perspective. To honor her final wishes, my husband and I quickly closed her modest apartment in Massachusetts and brought her to our home in Hawai'i for her remaining weeks of life.

As I have shared in earlier chapters, I have had many significant losses in my life but had never before been a caretaker for someone actively dying. It is a humbling experience that revealed every part of my small, selfish ego that wanted to run away from the intensity of death and impending loss. It challenged me in every moment to choose love instead of fear, dismay, and exhaustion. But sharing Mom's journey into death was an experience I would not trade for anything. From the unpleasant reality of changing the diaper of the person who had given birth to me, to the resplendent moment of witnessing her withdraw consciously from the physical body, those two weeks of life and death were rich with learning about how to love.

Because Mom and I had several weeks for closure, we talked about everything—what we were grateful for, what we regretted. Fortunately, we had the time and the awareness to leave nothing unsaid. I particularly remember a conversation with a hospice chaplain one day who asked us to share what we had learned from one another. Mom answered, "My daughter taught me how to love." In tears, I told her how grateful I was for the unconditional motherly love she had always given me.

Another transformative moment came as I was walking her to the bathroom one morning and she paused midway to take my face gently in her hands. At that point, she was not completely coherent, but she drew herself together in a moment of clarity, looked into my eyes, and said, "Your hair looks nice." This simple comment registered so significantly because Mom had always been critical of my hairstyles. This was a huge moment of acceptance for her. I knew then that how I wore my hair no longer mattered to her in the way it seemed to have in the past. She was seeing me through eyes of love, so I looked perfect as I was. I believe this was a healing moment for her, and it certainly was a moment of presence and visibility I will always cherish.

For me, the most powerful moment of opening into love came after a meditation at her bedside. I had been praying for release from some old resentment, and suddenly I felt myself let go of all expectation that she should be different than how she was. I fully and finally accepted her as the imperfect mom she had been and knew that she had done the very best she knew how to do. Even though her efforts had fallen short of what I needed at times, I recognized the effort and intention in her loving and was able to let go and forgive her shortcomings. This acceptance freed me from a lifetime of unfulfilled desire. When I looked at her frail and dying body, I no longer wished I could get some measure of love I needed from her. I only saw her inner being, her soul's light, and her heart's love.

In her last two days, she became mostly unresponsive as her spirit readied for transition out of physical form. I would sit near her to meditate and pray for a peaceful release from her body and my release from sadness. I had been postponing a trip I had planned before her diagnosis, and she knew that the time was drawing near for my final opportunity to depart. I was ready to let the trip go, of course, but I also knew she was ready to let go so I had not cancelled the plans.

On the day my flight was booked, I could sense her breathing slowing significantly. I felt a change in her energy, so I took her hand and began surrounding her with peace and love. She had a very special connection with my husband and knew that he returned home each day right around four p.m. It was close to that hour, and I was hoping he would not be late. The garage door opened at exactly four p.m. and I waved to him to come quickly. He went to the side of the bed and took her other hand. With both of us there beaming her love, she took three final breaths. We watched the energy withdraw from her feet to her head in a wave of unbelievable intention. The mother I had known and loved was gone, onward to other dimensions and experiences no doubt in greater awareness of love.

To say that I felt no sorrow would be untrue—I missed her from that very moment. I was terribly sad that I could no longer embrace or talk directly with the soul I had loved as mother in this lifetime. But I knew she was not gone from me in the greater experience of love. I felt her more completely there than ever before, more purely than I ever had while she was in human form because so much gets distorted by personality and the ego self.

In the months that followed her passing, every time my heart turned toward sorrow and loss, I remembered a saying that mom used to quote from Mary Baker Eddy about how divine love always has met and always will meet every human need. I know this to be true because every time I think it, love finds me and buoys me up. I know without a shadow of a doubt that Mom and I are never far apart in love.

Daily Practices

Compassionate Listening Exercise

You can do this for yourself or for another. Listen with an open heart and your full presence. Do not offer any advice, or opinions—just listen. When the person has completely finished sharing, simply ask: "Is there anything I can do to help?"

Reflection Before Dying

Given that death is inevitable and you will someday be asking yourself these questions, why not consider them now?

- What have I done with my life?

- Am I happy with what I have done?

- What am I doing to give my life meaning?

- What am I doing to create a legacy of love?

- Am I spending my time, energy, and resources wisely?

- What needs completing in my life?

- Who do I need to forgive?

- From whom do I need to ask forgiveness?

- What will help me in the final moment?

- What can I do now to prepare for death?

- How can I strengthen my mind now to be ready to face death consciously?

- Can I love today as if there will be no tomorrow?

Reflection on Deathlessness

You are a divine being made of the energy of love. Your bodily form will change, but you will not be gone. Reflecting upon this, how does it alter how you feel about physical death?

Chapter Fifteen

....

Imagining a New Reality

Love is the only reality and it is not
a mere sentiment. It is the ultimate
truth that lies at the heart of creation.
Rabindranath Tagore

We are nearing the end of our journey together. Like everything else in this physical world, this book will come to a close,
and we will all face the ongoing challenge of practicing love in
our own circles of influence. As we have seen, this pursuit is not
for the weak or passive. Nothing less than full commitment to
a higher order of things will do. The nerve cells of humanity
are raw with anxiety, fear, and separatism right now; spiritual
warriors are being called into action. If we succeed at loving
one another with enough intensity and devotion, we might
just calm things down in order to thrive as one beautiful world
family. For this to happen, we must dream into reality a new
paradigm of living and relating based on love.

Redefining Reality

I know many would say that for the whole human race to even *tolerate* one another is a long shot, but to coexist in love is downright *unrealistic*. This is because we typically define reality based on the beliefs of the time and place in which we live, which are the result of the consciousness of those who came before us. This perpetuates a self-fulfilling prophecy of the same experiences yet again.

It only takes a glance back in history, however, to recognize that the possibilities of creation far exceed our capacity to grasp them at any given time. Not everything we think or have been taught is true, and even if something *seems* true right now, that does not mean it will remain so a year from now. Over time, what we know to be true changes, as does what we know to be possible. Humans used to believe the world was flat and the earth revolved around the sun! Defining moments of discovery have turned the prevailing theory of reality upside-down and backward numerous times.

A New Paradigm Needed

When collective awareness expands, suddenly nothing is seen in the same way again. This is why questioning what we accept as real is a powerful consciousness-expanding practice we should undertake both personally and cooperatively. When it comes to love, we need to challenge the assumptions that make up our existing worldview and open ourselves to new possibilities.

To expand beyond the currently accepted reality requires that we stop operating from habitual thinking long enough to allow new perceptions to enter our awareness, which is why meditation is the essential practice to initiate transformation. It allows us to transcend personal thought temporarily and perceive something beyond what we have previously experienced. When we reenter our cognitive process, we bring with us new inspirations from the field of potential, including the ability to create a new reality based in love.

To step beyond what is known into what can be, such as a vision of the world where the majority of people live according to the principle of love, we must employ the energy of imagination. Imagination is the process of tapping into what exists beyond the known boundaries of accepted truth. Albert Einstein said that imagination is *more important than* intellect and credited it as essential to his discoveries.

By forming a mental image of something not present to the senses through our imaginations, we creatively deal with challenge. Engaging imagination in relation to love, we access the field of the great Self's potential, actualizing what has lain dormant and unconscious within us.

I would say it is high time we use our collective imagination to shift from our survivalist, fear-based reality paradigm to a cooperative, love-based one. The current mode of operating from distrust and hatred is proving detrimental to the future of our planet, not to mention our personal happiness. Love is the creative key to resolving our problems, and enabling us to become a sustainable and unified human family.

Harnessing the Energy of Love

Metaphysicians have always understood that we have the power to manage and move energy and that we do so both consciously and unconsciously. When quantum physicists explained that matter is actually *all* energy, it became easier to understand that we have an incredible force to utilize as we wish, and that we best do so with consciousness and responsibility to the highest good. To direct our incredibly potent energy in a positive direction, we must remain humble and motivated by love in our thoughts, choices, and actions.

The energetic principles of the universe are indiscriminate; anything we direct belief and will force toward, we will be given. Like electricity that runs through either a blender or a lamp, there is no difference in the source of the energy, only its conduit. We are the ultimate energy channels, so it will manifest through us in whatever way we direct it, through our consciousness of fear or our consciousness of love.

This phenomenon is often described as the law of attraction or the law of manifestation. Whatever we think of often, expect on the deepest level, and imagine most vividly will come to be. Form follows idea, so if we want to see more love in the world, *we* have to choose more loving thoughts and actions *now*.

To enter a new reality, we must challenge *all* beliefs and assumptions we hold that are not loving. We must self-reflect and notice how we withhold love from others or from ourselves. Every time our egos try to block love with opinions, defenses, and fears, we must instead choose humility and be willing to surrender our positions of perceived rightness.

Any beliefs we discover that do not serve the highest good are not ones from which we want to create a future reality— like using today's garbage to make tomorrow's feast. We must choose instead a fresh commitment to love that fuels authentic connection in all our relationships. We need to use our will to affirm the ultimate reality of love and cultivate the feeling within that it is already manifest in our lives. As we maintain an unwavering devotion to expanding love, living as if it was already our reality, it will become so.

Energy focused in this way stokes a brilliant fire of transformation within individual hearts and the world at large. Clearly, we cannot rely solely on our intellects, because if we could have *figured out* how to love more through the mind, we would have done so by now. Reason does not win hearts. Love does.

We all share the silent intuitive awareness beyond reason, and it is through meditation and imagination that we access this miraculous realm where love knows exactly what to do. Here we move beyond our previously conceived limitations and expand into the vast potential of love. Here we find the way to relate to one another in peace and harmony.

Through deeper absorption into love in meditation and every conscious breath of love we share with one another, we start to neutralize the pervasive fear and negativity that have been the norm. We perceive that beneath all the anger and hatred is actually a deep sadness and longing for what we have collectively forgotten. Beneath the longing and sadness is the love that brings us back together. Coming home to our Self in this way, we find that any lack and conflict can be overcome.

Opening to Greater Potential

Our point of power is in *this present moment*. Every thought we think is a magnet. Hate or blessing, it is our choice and returns to us in the same equal measure. If we choose love now, we can move beyond the limitations and losses of the past.

Instead of fearing, ruminating, or resenting, whenever we have a free moment we can dwell on a thought of love. This practice will become our living meditation if we discipline our minds to focus on the beautiful, the true, and the loving, spiritualizing thought at every turn.

Of course if serious depression, anxiety, or mental illness are present we should address these concerns with a medical professional to get help in managing the thoughts we hold onto and the actions they fuel. Even if we succeed at converting just one worry into a consistent thought of love, it will make a huge difference in our happiness, and in the wellbeing of those around us.

Obviously, the daily effort required to approach every circumstance with love is not to be underestimated. This commitment is not easy for anyone. It is a dedication that requires constant watchfulness of our tendency to slip back into closed-heartedness, self-centeredness, doubt, and fear. It requires willingness to show up again and again, to give more than we think we have to give.

The Dharma of Love

If we hope to create a reality of higher love, we cannot base our behavior on that of others or be concerned with whether they are expressing love. Love asks that we stretch past our comfort zones, past the places where we are tired of giving or do not feel we have it in us to do so. We must love with no expectation for return, and accept that even when we succeed, there may only be a handful of hearts that respond.

Love requires that we mine the most tender wounds of our hearts to find ever deeper veins of compassion and strength, regardless of the pain of the past. It asks that we pour our hearts into every interaction, every relationship, and every communication. We must love even when we do not feel like it—*especially* when we do not feel like it.

We will not succeed one hundred percent of the time. But whatever we do today is *enough,* because every effort in love is a tremendous force that blesses everyone.

The Ultimate Reality

Why should we go to this effort, when it seems easier to wait and hope that love will find us, choose us, or heal us? Because this is the purpose of life, to awaken the love within our hearts, and to reconnect our individual consciousness with the divine Source of love. Only this will bring us bliss.

Everything in the material world changes and passes away, so it cannot be the final truth. That which is *eternal* is, and love is eternal. Therefore love is the ultimate reality, the most *real* experience we share as human beings.

So no more excuses, no more blame, no more hiding, posturing, defending, or hoping that someone else will do it for us. Let us commit wholeheartedly to the practice of breathing love today.

A Personal Story

There was a time in my life when I felt so much emotional pain from the losses I had endured that I thought it would be easier just to die rather than continuing living in such anguish. I felt adrift from hope and faith and love. The dark night of my soul had descended.

To make sense of my own experience at the time, I was studying a form of body-centered therapy, learning the ways our emotional experiences affect our physical bodies. In the program, my classmates and I used one another as models for the material we were studying, and we were each undergoing a year of intense personal therapy as a result.

One night it was my turn to stand before the class and share a particularly vulnerable and painful experience that was keeping me blocked. In addition to having to tell the story aloud, I was handed a baseball bat and positioned before a punching bag to physically act out my feelings. Throughout my sharing, the facilitator prompted me to go deeper, asking questions that drew forth the emotional memories associated with the experience I was recounting. Tears began to flow, and she instructed me to hit the punching bag with the bat.

I felt drained by the storytelling and had little energy to strike the bag. I did it as a matter of course until I could move no more and collapsed on my knees, a sobbing mess. I felt so weary of the fight in life. The teacher paused for a moment and then asked, "So is that it? Are you done?"

On the floor, with my face buried in my hands, I asked myself, "Am I *done?*" This question pierced my heart like some kind of arrow from the ethers, and suddenly I felt a surge of energy shoot through me like never before. Rising from my puddle of tears like a phoenix from the ashes, I stood up and began pummeling the punching bag with a superhuman force that had appeared within me from some unknown source. I let out a scream so intense that I did not recognize my own sound. "NO! I am not *done*. I will *not* give up. I do not care if I am tested until my dying day, I will *not* give in to this darkness. I will *not* give up. I will *not* give up on love."

I am not sure how long my screaming went on, but it was as though a vein of power had been tapped inside me that had been blocked up until that moment. I absolutely *knew* then that nothing would be the same again. I would not be the victim of circumstance. I would not allow the pain within me or around me to obscure the light I wanted to shine into the world. The critics and unkind people I encountered would no longer discourage me. I knew the power of love within me would overcome whatever difficulty might come my way.

That day, I felt a new commitment to joy arise—in fact, nothing has been the same since then. Many of the stories

I have shared here in these pages are a result of that whole-hearted turning toward love. Looking back, I feel nothing but gratitude for that dark night of the soul because it forced me to make a choice: to create a reality of love in every way I knew how. My choice has informed every aspect of my life, work, relationships, and parenting since.

At the time, my son was four years old and stuck in a terrible pattern of negative thinking. When I pulled myself out of my own depression, I realized I needed to set a strong example for him as to how to live love. I did not want to see his life steered by negativity or fear. To do this, I had to walk my talk about love, and I have shared with you here the process I have been through and continue to practice on a daily basis.

Many years have passed, and we are now just days away from his eighteenth birthday. I must have done something right because he is one of the most positive thinkers I know, and that is not easy for most teenagers. When he sees me get discouraged, he gives me pep talks and reminds me of the very things I taught him. He shares his feelings and frustrations about living an open-hearted life in a world that is not always supportive. And he hugs me every day—big, real hugs filled with love. I am so grateful.

The other night he told me that he, like many of his peers, was considering getting a tattoo, something I have mixed feelings about. I asked him what he wanted a tattoo of, and he replied, "Mom, I want it to say, 'Choose Love.'" Guess I can't argue with that!

Daily Practices

Watching the Heart

As you interact with different people throughout your day, notice if your heart feels open or closed. Make a conscious choice to open it again and again, even in difficult situations. Create new dynamic relationships based on love. And always keep your heart open, no matter what.

Serving Love

Set an intention to serve love in some tangible way today. Volunteer your time to help someone in need. Send silent blessings to homeless people you see. See someone through eyes of love. Forgive yourself or someone else. Never miss an opportunity to love.

Love Flooding

Think of the people you love the most. Make a list of all the things you love about them. Share this with them just because. Next, think of someone you do not like so much. Make a list of all the ways you could extend love to them. Give at least one a try.

Make Love Your Reality Exercise

Throughout the book, we have identified ways to practice loving more. Now consider the following list of ways to create a new reality based completely in love.

- Rise above negative and hurt feelings and practice calm silent loving presence. Maintain evenness of mind.

- Be sensitive to the feelings of others and less touchy about your own.

- Do not take things personally. See situations from the other person's point of view. By all means do not demand perfection, which you yourself cannot give.

- Accept and love people as they are, and do not give advice that is not explicitly requested.

- Identify fearful or love-limiting beliefs. Counter them by affirming love as the most powerful force of creation, greater than any fear or limitation.

- Commit to making decisions from love not fear.

- If you encounter thoughtlessness, meanness, or criticism, reflect on these qualities within yourself first. Then respond in love using only genuinely kind and courteous language. Whatever you have to say, say it with love.

- Do not dwell on failure. See every setback as another opportunity to open your heart to more love.

- Build resilience and commitment to love by throwing out negative thoughts. Negativity creates suffering and separates you from love. Choose to hold onto only love-activating thoughts.

- Be unselfish, kind, and understanding to everyone around you.

- Be grateful constantly. Express appreciation to people in your life.

- Be compassionate with yourself and others.

- Visualize love manifesting in your life in ever-expanding ways.

Imagination Meditation

At the end of your daily meditation, when the mind is quiet and the heart is open, imagine a world in which people interacted in love all the time. Really let yourself go to the extreme. Visualize the course of your own day flowing with ease as you speak to each person with generosity and kindness, and them returning the same openness and compassion to you. We create from our imagination, so let yours dwell on love. The more clearly and completely you envision this possibility, the greater chance you have of making it your reality. Write down your vision of a reality based on love.

Build Your Love Consciousness

Regardless of your life circumstances at this moment, you can effect positive change by committing to faithful daily exercise of your *will to love*. Begin today to purify your mind from anything contrary to it. Reject wholeheartedly every thought of judgment, criticism, resentment, hatred, pride, or prejudice. Root out from your heart every speck of anything that is not an expression of love, and do not give in to emotions of fear, anger, envy, lust, or selfishness. Not only will your personal difficulties begin to clear, but you will also effect a magnitude of good for the human race.

Conclusion

The only thing that matters, at the end
of a stay on earth, is how well did we love.
Richard Bach

Love is life's blood and if we want to really live, loving must be our mission. Whether we do this in large or small ways, whether we struggle with the choice or find it easy, love is always worth it in the end. The daily action of *loving* takes us to the state of *being* love and this is the most joyful place of all. There is no greater purpose we can assign to our lives than to love everyone who crosses our path, as totally and as unconditionally as we possibly can. And nothing will bring us more happiness than this.

The following tenets of love are listed to help you remember the most important principles. Secure them deep in your heart, and wherever you are in life with whomever you find yourself right now, choose love. Then keep on breathing love, no matter what.

Ten Tenets of Love

1. You can never be separated from love because it is who you *are*. Love is your true nature.

2. All personal love you experience and express is a part of the one Source love.

3. The love you seek is around and within you now. You are deeply loved.

4. Meditation reconnects you to the love that waits within your own being.

5. The more you live and breathe love, the happier you will become.

6. Every challenge is an opportunity to choose and practice greater love.

7. Forgiveness is another word for love.

8. Regardless of how others behave, keep your heart open and love anyway.

9. Love is the greatest power of all. Only love can heal the world.

10. When your love becomes greater than your pain, your life will be transformed.

PART THREE

....

Appendices

....

Appendix One:
A Meditation to Experience
the Love That You Are

This meditation guides you into a relaxed ability to expand awareness beyond the small self and to connect with the greater Self that is pure love. Good to practice anytime you need to get centered, increase your capacity to give or receive, or connect with the essence of your own being. It can be recorded to play to yourself or read out loud to another.

Find a quiet place where you will not be disturbed. Settle into a comfortable position, making sure that you feel supported and completely at ease. Allow your body to relax and get still. Turn your attention to the natural breath as it rises and falls. Just notice for a few moments how it feels to breathe. (Pause)

If your eyes are not already closed, gently close them now and allow your attention to drift inward. Set the intention that you are here to connect to your heart and to the love that lives within your own being.

Begin to regulate your breath into a slower, steadier rhythm. Breathe in calmness and breathe out tension. Slow down even more. Calmness in. Tension out. Notice anything present in this moment, any feelings or sensations, any thoughts or desires. Simply watch these impulses rise and fall like waves rolling in at the shoreline.

Gently place one or both hands on your chest. Sense the breath moving in and out of this space. Tune in to the rhythmic beating of your heart. Just be present with your self and listen to anything your heart has to share, no judgment, no analysis. Just acceptance. Just being. (Pause)

Now transfer your attention from the senses and nerves around the physical heart center, deeper inward to the energetic space of the spiritual heart. Pull all your awareness inside and completely withdraw from the external world. Free yourself from the tug of your outer life, and get ready to contact the love that is waiting within. (Pause)

Focus your complete attention in the area of the heart. Imagine your breath is flowing in and out of this center, pulsing in bigger and bigger waves. Beneath all your thoughts and feelings, waiting for the waves to settle, is love. It is the deepest well of your being, the essence of who you are. The supply is infinite, endless, and ever-renewing, like a stream of fresh pure joy.

Feel the fullness of love that is you, bubbling through every cell of your body. It radiates within you in every direction and out from you in ever-expanding spheres. As you rest here, the river of love replenishes you in every way—with willpower, creativity, compassion, vitality, understanding, patience, and joy. It prepares you to open more completely to life today, helping you choose nourishing activities, attract positive friends, eat healthy foods, and enjoy inspiring environments. It enables you to remain calm, even in challenging moments, and to serve in increasingly easeful ways. This vibration of love lightens your spirit and sustains you and everyone around you, multiplying itself through every breath.

Freedom and expansion replace any sense of restriction or limitation. Doubt clears, and faith takes its place. All limiting beliefs fall away and you feel the spaciousness of pure love within. Immersed in the pulsing field of loving energy, you feel connected to your most precious Self. You are breathing love and you are being breathed by love. The sacred is within you. It is you. Rest here, still in the presence of love. (Pause)

When you feel ready, gently return your awareness to the sensation of the breath rising and falling in the chest. Notice how open your heart feels. Appreciate that you can always return to this awareness of your Self as love. For now, fill your mind with thoughts of gratitude and goodwill for yourself or someone else. Make an internal commitment to re-enter your day from this place of connectedness in love. Gently blink your eyes open and smile. *You are love.*

Appendix Two:
A Meditation for Letting Go Into Love

This meditation facilitates relaxation, the ability to release fear, and trust that you are always inside love. Whether you are feeling stuck, moving through a life transition, nearing death, or supporting someone else at the end of life; this meditation will help you trust the process and let go gently into love. It can be recorded to play to yourself or read out loud to another.

Find a quiet place away from distractions. Settle into a comfortable position, making sure that you feel supported and completely at ease. Allow your body to relax and get still. Turn your attention to the natural breath as it rises and falls. Just notice for a few moments how it feels to breathe. (Pause)

Notice any places in the body or the mind that may be holding tension. Direct your breath to those places and relax even more. Start to deepen the breath and continue sending each slow, full breath into the places that feel tight or tense. Tell yourself that it is time to relax completely. There is nowhere to go, nothing to do, nothing to analyze or solve. It is just time to rest. Continue this for several minutes until you relax into a state of calm presence and awareness. (Pause)

Now allow your breathing to return to its natural rhythm. Do not attempt to control the breath in any way. Just focus on the moment by moment coming and going of the breath with no special effort. Feel the heaviness of the physical body as it releases into the support beneath it. The body, relaxed and heavy. Just being. Thoughts may arise but then they move on.

Gently turn your internal gaze upward to the point between the eyebrows, the center of intuitive wisdom and guidance. Without straining in any way, focus on whatever you see within and enter the deep space of inner stillness. This is a space of peace. Here there is nothing to accomplish, just spacious, soft awareness, rising and passing away. Here, you exist in the flow of being and in the expansiveness of love.

Just be here. Just be now. Relax into deeper and deeper being, aware of the vast love around you and within you. Nothing to do. Nowhere to go. Every effort dropping away. All doing, holding, forcing, resisting, just melts away with the gentle breath. Sense the energy of spirit within the physical body, light and free.

Now feel the breath moving in and out from the center of the chest. Breathe into your heart space. Breathe naturally and just be with whatever you feel. Place one or both hands on the heart center and take a breath of deep acceptance for all that is present. As you breathe, acceptance grows and is joined by compassion—acceptance and compassion for all that is now and all that has been, acceptance and compassion for yourself and for all those in your life. Move even deeper into the spaciousness created by acceptance and compassion. (Pause)

Here, in this still place of compassionate awareness, all restlessness subsides. Here you know that you are not the sensations that rise and fall away. You are not your thoughts, and you are not your feelings. You are not the experiences that have happened in your life. No more "I," "me," or "mine." No more "I am responsible for," "I have to," "I should," or "I will." You are the spacious awareness that exists beyond all of these. Just you being. Being love.

Detaching from the physical body, detaching from the analytical mind, detaching from the emotional waves and all worldly concerns. Sense the freedom that exists as you expand beyond these limitations. Experience the lightness of love flowing and changing within you. All identification with the outer self fading into the background. Feel the energy of love that is you. Silently remind yourself, "I am *love*. I *am* love. *I* am love." (Pause)

Now imagine your soul's light gathered there as a small radiant orb of glimmering white light. As you breathe, it grows brighter and brighter, and as it does, it starts spreading luminosity throughout your whole body. This is the energy of pure love, filling up the container of the physical body with your expansive spirit. The light of love glows in your heart and beams outward from it. It shines through your eyes and moves through your senses. This is the essence of love that has always been in you. It exists in the deep spaciousness of your heart and guides your every breath.

As this love light travels through your body, it clears away any restrictions, any places of tension or pain. It continues to expand beyond your physical body, illuminating the energy field around you, purifying and protecting you. It permeates all the space as far as you can imagine. Rest here in this spacious, peaceful awareness. (Pause)

All is love. You are inside love. You are love, now and forever more.

Appendix Three:
Affirmations of Love

Think of these affirmations like little love sparks. In order to move the creative force of love into manifestation, affirmations should be practiced with intensity of feeling and faith. Cast away all worry, fear, and doubt. Let your heart, not your mind, speak these words of love. Connect to your heart center as you repeat them audibly with increasing volume, then again more softly, and then mentally with unbroken concentration.

I go to the quiet place within. Here I connect to love.

I am the energy of pure love, strength, and joy.

I am ever surrounded and protected by all-powerful love.

All my choices and actions come from love.

I breathe love in. I breathe love out. Love is who I am.

My being is anchored in a deep trust of love.

The power of love enlivens me and enables me to handle any challenge life brings.

I speak and act from calm, loving openness.

Love flows through me in an easeful, generous way.

I show up in love day by day.

My breath flows with love, infusing every cell of my body.

I consciously create my present moment reality through loving thoughts and actions.

I am free to choose a reality of love.

I choose to live with an open heart.

I look for love and find it everywhere.

I respond to all situations in a loving and compassionate way.

I communicate truth with love and gentleness.

I allow my love to blaze fearlessly.

I am filled with love and share it freely with all those who cross my path.

I care for my body so that it may be a vibrant vessel of love.

I hold myself in love and understanding.

I am guided by love.

I am always, innately worthy of love.

Life is unfolding as it should, full of opportunities to love.

I am surrounded by love.

I place myself in love's gentle care.

I am open and receptive to all love and wisdom.

I am receiving all the love I need.

I know my Self as love.

Love shines through me in ever greater measure.

I feel and know love as safety, provision, and protection.

I have instant access to love at all times because it lives within me.

I am valued and appreciated by love.

I expand love's expression through understanding and compassion.

I am peace. I am joy. I am love.

Appendix Four:
Prayers of Love

Prayer is any offering of love from our hearts, in the language of our souls. It can be based in gratitude, surrender, awe, or a request for support and guidance. In the stillness of meditation lies the perfect opportunity to present our prayers to love on the altar of our devotion. Make up your own or modify the following to suit your own personal expression.

I call upon the great spirit of love that is within all creation. Open me. Clear me. Pour through me. Wash away anything that keeps me from seeing myself as love. Break down my self-limitations. Free me from the bondage of fear, temptation, and anger. Quiet my thoughts. Expand my heart. Make me open and light. Fill me with your healing energy today.

· · · · · · · · · · · · · ·

Love, help me to know that you are all around me and within me always. Show me how to see myself and everyone through eyes of love, remembering our unity. Help me to awaken my heart and the hearts of others. Make my words and my hands instruments of healing. Help me to give selflessly and to remember that I exist in pure joy, pure peace, now and forever.

. . . .

Thank you love. Thank you for leading my mind and my soul, my will and my intention, to their highest and most authentic place. May others find hope through my words and my actions. May they find comfort and faith. May I serve you through all that I do. May I be a healing presence in the world. Make me always a willing channel for your endless expression. Show me how to serve the shifting of consciousness toward more unity between all people.

. . . .

I trust you love, your light, your provision, your magnificence. I trust your doors; those that open and those that close. I trust your way. Thank you for giving me strength to give and receive freely and abundantly every day, in greater and greater ways.

Recommended Resources

Bach, Richard. *Illusions: The Adventures of a Reluctant Messiah.* New York: Delacorte Press, 1977.

Bolsta, Phil. *Through God's Eyes: Finding Peace and Purpose in a Troubled World.* Willow River, MN: James Monroe Publishing, 2012.

Bouanchaud, Bernard. *The Essence of Yoga: Reflections on the Yoga Sutras of Patanjali.* Delhi, India: Indian Books Centre, 1997.

Brown, Brené. *Daring Greatly: How the Courage to Be Vulnerable Transforms the Way We Live, Love, Parent, and Lead.* New York: Avery, 2015.

Chopra, Deepak. *The Ultimate Happiness Prescription: 7 Keys to Joy and Enlightenment.* New York: Harmony Books, 2009.

Cohen, Alan. *A Course in Miracles Made Easy: Mastering the Journey from Fear to Love.* New York: Hay House, 2015.

Covey, Steven M. R. *The Speed of Trust: The One Thing That Changes* Everything. New York: Free Press, 2008.

Daleo, Morgan Simone. *Curriculum of Love: Cultivating the Spiritual Nature of Children.* Charlottesville, VA: Grace Publishing & Communications, 1996.

Dossey, Larry. *One Mind: How Our Individual Mind Is Part of a Greater Consciousness and Why It Matters.* New York: Hay House, 2013.

Easwaran, Eknath. *Gandhi the Man: The Story of His Transformation.* Berkeley, CA: Nilgiri Press, 1997.

Gandhi, M.K. *The Way to God.* Berkeley, CA: Berkeley Hills Books, 1999.

Gibran, Kahlil. *The Prophet.* New York: Alfred A. Knopf, 1978.

Hanh, Thich Nhat. *How To Love.* Berkeley, CA: Parallax Press, 2015.

Holden, Robert. *Loveability: Knowing How to Love and Be Loved.* New York: Hay House, 2013.

Jampolsky, Gerald. *Love is Letting Go of Fear.* New York: Crown Publishing, 1979.

Lake, Gina. *Loving in the Moment: Moving from Ego to Essence in Relationships.* New York: Endless Satsang Foundation, 2007.

Levine, Stephen. *A Gradual Awakening*. Norwell, MA: Anchor Press, 1989.

Mata, Sri Daya. *Only Love: Living the Spiritual Life in a Changing World*. Los Angeles: Self Realization Fellowship, 1976.

Merton, Thomas. *Love and Living*. New York: Harcourt Books, 1979.

Mood, John J. L. *Rilke on Love and Other Difficulties: Translations and Considerations of Rainer Maria Rilke*. New York: W.W. Norton & Co., 1975.

Myss, Carolyn. *Anatomy of the Spirit: The Seven Stages of Power and Healing*. New York: Three Rivers Press, 1996.

Nepo, Mark. *The Book of Awakening: Having the Life You Want by Being Present to the Life You Have*. San Francisco: Conari Press, 2000.

Post, Stephen, and Jill Neimark. *Why Good Things Happen to Good People: How to Live a Longer, Healthier, Happier Life by the Simple Act of Giving*. New York: Broadway Books, 2007.

Sarayu. *Being with Dying: A Practical Guide to Serving Others Through Times of Illness and Death*. Kerala, India: Mata Amritanandamayi Mission Trust, 2011.

Siegel, Bernie. *Peace, Love and Healing: Bodymind Communication & the Path to Self-Healing: An Exploration*. New York: Harper Collins, 1989.

Sinetar, Marsha. *Elegant Choices, Healing Choices.* New York: Paulist Press, 1988.

Singer, Michael. *The Untethered Soul: The Journey Beyond Yourself.* Oakland, CA: New Harbinger, 2007.

Spangler, David. *Blessing: The Art and the Practice.* New York: Riverhead Books, 2001.

Sparks Phylis. *Forgiveness ... It Is NOT What You Think It Is!* Bloomington, IN: Balboa Press, 2016.

Welwood, John. *Journey of the Heart: Intimate Relationship and the Path of Love.* New York: HarperPerennial, 1990.

Williamson, Marianne. *A Return to Love: Reflections on the Principles of a "Course in Miracles."* San Francisco: HarperOne, 1996.

Yogananda, Paramahansa. *Autobiography of a Yogi.* Los Angeles: Self Realization Fellowship, 1998.

———. *The Divine Romance: Collected Talks and Essays on Realizing God in Daily Life, Volumes II and III.* Los Angeles: Self Realization Fellowship, 2005.

Index

Acknowledgements

- Greatest gratitude to my guru Paramahansa Yogananda for being the shining example of pure love in my life.

- Countless hugs to my husband Larry for supporting me through the discouraging days, buying champagne to celebrate the winning days, and for being the best spiritual partner in life and in love every day.

- Awe and joy to my son Benen for growing into an incredible young man, for loving me always, and for helping me learn how to love unconditionally.

- Deepest appreciation to the team at Llewellyn for giving me the reins to run with this one.

- Blessings to my dear friend Lotta for supporting me and for the innumerable laughs about the difficulties of remaining devoted to the spiritual path.

- Peace and encouragement to everyone who practices meditation. Your efforts make a positive difference to the health of this world and our human family. May you completely realize your Self as love and may we meet each other in this heaven.

- Warm hugs to all the beautiful souls who have shared their personal love with me in this lifetime. You know who you are. Whether we are still connected, or estranged because of our ego failures, you are, every one, in my heart. You helped me learn what love is, and I am forever grateful. If you think of me, just remember me loving you. Let the rest go. Only love matters in the end.

About the Author

Jennie Lee (Hawaii) is a certified yoga therapist who has spent two decades coaching people in the healing tradition of classical yoga meditation. Using the practices she writes about in *Breathing Love*, Jennie helps people overcome grief, depression, anxiety, and stress as well as create lives filled with greater joy. Author of the award-winning book *True Yoga*, Jennie's writing has also been featured in dozens of wellness blogs and magazines including the *Huffington Post, Mind Body Green, Yoga Digest,* and *Yogi Times.* She counsels via phone or Skype internationally and from her home studio on the island of O'ahu. Visit her online at www.JennieLeeYogaTherapy.com.

Praise for *Breathing Love*

"Brilliant, elegant, and easily practical for those just getting into meditation, and for the seasoned veteran. This is a book to cherish, filled with good stories from Jennie's remarkable life of devotion." —Stephen G. Post, author of *Why Good Things Happen to Good People* and president of the Institute for Research on Unlimited Love

"This book will set you on the path to healing and to seeing relationships in a whole new light. Through her personal stories, Lee illustrates the way we can evolve consciousness from fear to love—an essential skill for everyone's inner peace."
—Gerald G. Jampolsky, MD,
co-author of *Aging with Attitude*

"*Breathing Love* will grant you a widening connection to your purest love and your true Self."   —Elena Brower, author of *Art of Attention* and *Practice You*

"I love Jennie Lee's rallying cry to choose love anyway, always, and no matter what. She will show you how to break open your heart and let the love that's inside you, the love that is your very essence, pour forth into the world and bless everyone it touches."   —Phil Bolsta, author of *Through God's Eyes*

"*Breathing Love* is an important book, which shows us how to fulfill the need that connects us all as human beings ... Those who read Jennie's words, take them into their hearts, and put them into practice will be living the fullest, most meaningful and purpose-driven life possible."
—Scarlett Lewis, president and founder
of the Jesse Lewis Choose Love Movement

"This book will help each one of us fulfill our ultimate purpose and live in what can only be called a heaven on earth."
—Cherie Healey, Possibilitarian